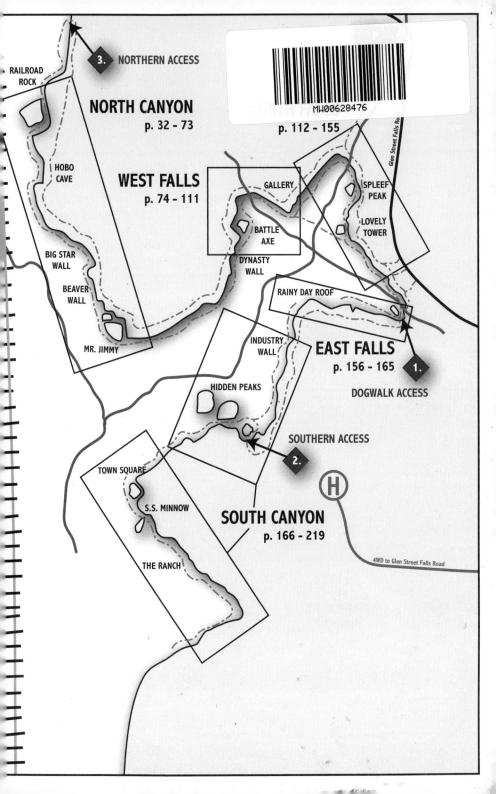

RAILROAD
ROCK

3. NORTHERN ACCESS

NORTH CANYON
p. 32 – 73

p. 112 – 155

MW00628476

HOBO
CAVE

WEST FALLS
p. 74 – 111

GALLERY

SPLEEF
PEAK

LOVELY
TOWER

BIG STAR
WALL

BATTLE
AXE

BEAVER
WALL

DYNASTY
WALL

RAINY DAY ROOF

MR. JIMMY

INDUSTRY
WALL

EAST FALLS
p. 156 – 165

1.

DOGWALK ACCESS

HIDDEN PEAKS

SOUTHERN ACCESS

2.

TOWN SQUARE

(H)

S.S. MINNOW

SOUTH CANYON
p. 166 – 219

THE RANCH

4WD to Glen Street Falls Road

Glen Street Falls Rd

JACKSON FALLS

A GUIDE TO SOUTHERN ILLINOIS' BEST KEPT SECRET

THIS BOOK BELONGS TO

Jackson Falls

by Yusuf Daneshyar

Published and distributed by Brayackmedia Publishing.
www.brayackmedia.com
Dan Brayack
brayackmedia@gmail.com

Brayackmedia Publishing

ISBN: 978-0-9907821-0-0

Cover Page Photo: p. 178. Patti Zdanowski on Detox Mountain 5.12a. Photo Matthew P. Guempel.
Title Page Photo: p. 63. Tom Herstenstein on Frizzle Fry 5.12b. Photo Kevin Sierzega.

Cover Design: Taylor Ashford
Map Designs: Sophie Binder

Words: Yusuf Daneshyar
Topo/Rock Images: Dan Brayack unless noted.
Maps: Yusuf Daneshyar
Overview Map: Sophie Binder
Editing and Design: Dan Brayack - Brayackmedia Publishing, Yusuf Daneshyar
Printed in China.

If you have a book project & would like to publish it with Brayackmedia - contact Dan Brayack -
brayackmedia@gmail.com I will pay you really well and would love to love your awesome area!

WARNING:

Immediately burn this guidebook and read no further unless you agree to the following:

Rock Climbing and Bouldering is inherently dangerous. Information in this guide may not be accurate and may lead to dangerous situations. A significant degree of experience is needed to rock climb and instruction in such is outside the scope of this guidebook. It is recommended that each climber take a separate safety instruction class before using this guidebook.

There are many hazards and dangers that are not described in this book and the authors and publishers of this book provide no guarantee that the information in this book is accurate.

The user of this book assumes all risk associated with rock climbing. Be careful out there ok?

p. 91. Alex Beyer climbing The Reckoning 5.12a. Photo Dan Brayack.

ROCK CANDY
HOLDS

SUPPORT YOUR LOCAL ROUTE SETTER

www.rockcandyholds.com

TABLE OF CONTENTS

p. 181. Jessica Joganic on Cheerio Bowl 5.10a on Pricker Peak. Photo Yusuf Daneshyar.

p. 238. Kristi Ganz on Remove La Ropa 5.12b. Photo Kevin Sierzega.

BETAFUND

PRESERVE. EDUCATE. INSPIRE.

The BETA Fund provides a unified voice for climbers in the Midwestern region through environmental advocacy, educational campaigning, and community service.

WWW.BETAFUND.ORG

ROUTE GRADES

A considerable effort was made in this guidebook to present the climbing at Jackson Falls accurately. The grades included in this book are based on the experience of local climbers and were assigned relative to the other routes in the canyon. As with any climbing destination, there is a learning curve and those unfamiliar with the style of climbing at Jackson Falls will undoubtedly find it more challenging. Keep in mind that the grades suggested in this book are not hard figures. The difficulty of any given route is subject to change based on a variety of factors including weather conditions, the sequence used by the climber, and limitations or advantages based on body composition. That being said, treat the grades in this book as flexible figures and not concrete facts. Be open to trying routes based on your level of interest and not solely on what you think you might be capable of accomplishing during your visit.

Grades in this book have been color coded as a way to help users identify grade distribution more easily. Each color describes a range and individual routes are plotted on overview maps to help users determine which areas suit the needs and abilities of their party.

GUIDEBOOK ELEMENTS

On overview maps, cliff sunshine and shade times are given. These change throughout the year based on the sun angle so take these with a grain of salt. These designations do not take into account tree shade.

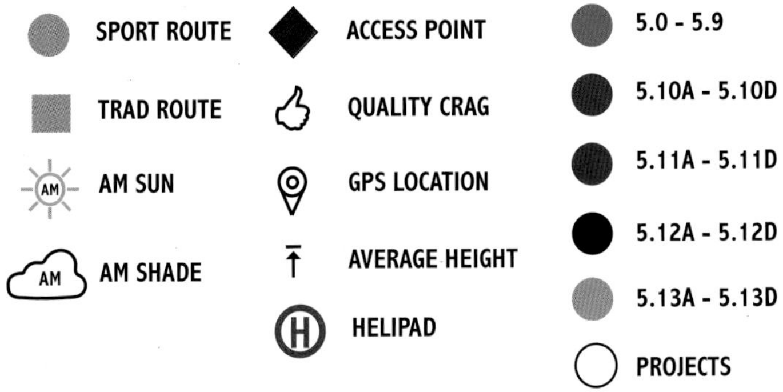

● SPORT ROUTE	◆ ACCESS POINT	● 5.0 - 5.9
■ TRAD ROUTE	👍 QUALITY CRAG	● 5.10A - 5.10D
☀ AM SUN	◉ GPS LOCATION	● 5.11A - 5.11D
☁ AM SHADE	� AVERAGE HEIGHT	● 5.12A - 5.12D
	Ⓗ HELIPAD	● 5.13A - 5.13D
		○ PROJECTS

STARS

A star system has been included in order to help visitors quickly identify quality routes. This system is a representation of collective opinions regarding the quality of routes found in the area. The star system may be helpful in guiding you toward routes that you will enjoy, but should only be used as a loose reference. In the end you may fall in love with a one-star route and wonder why it didn't receive three-stars.

NO-STAR — A route that does not receive any stars likely has no redeeming qualities making it worth the time or effort to climb. If you are short on time, it would be in your best interest to find another route. There are a lot to choose.

★ — A one-star route may offer some enjoyable climbing, but has one or more detracting features including heinous holds, clumsy movement, poor rock quality or limited height.

★★ — A two-star route provides enjoyable climbing but might have a single-move crux or natural hindrances (like seepage) preventing it from receiving a higher rating.

★★★ — A three-star route is a solid, worthwhile climb that is reasonably popular among locals but lacks replay value. In other words, this route is worth climbing once but does not have enough character to revisit.

★★★★ — Four-star routes have good height, consistent challenges, aesthetic physical characteristics and unique moves. These are among the most trafficked climbs in the canyon and have a high replay value.

★★★★★ — A five-star route at Jackson Falls is a classic that exemplifies quality rock climbing in the area. These routes have it all: sculpted holds, exciting movement, unique features, scenic location, and historical significance. The routes that fall into this category are gems that make Jackson Falls a climbing destination worth visiting.

LOCATION

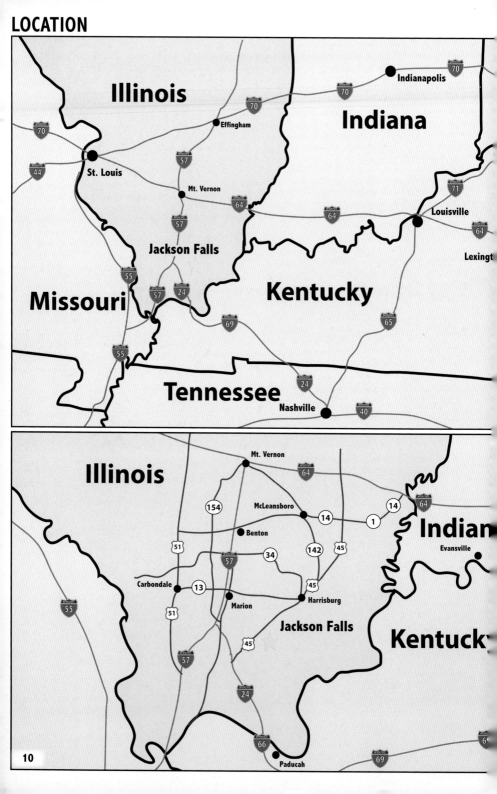

DIRECTIONS

Jackson Falls is located in Southern Illinois approximately 50 miles East of Carbondale, IL and 30 miles South of Harrisburg, IL. The closest town to Jackson Falls is Ozark, IL.

The GPS coordinates for the parking lot are 37°30'32.42" N, 88°40'54.75" W.

Individuals using a GPS device for driving directions should set their device to "Drive on un-paved roads."

DIRECTIONS TO OZARK, IL FROM THE NORTH/NORTHWEST

Make your way to I-24 and take I-24 East. Continue along East along I-24 and take Exit 7 toward Tunnel Hill Road & Goreville.

At the stop sign, turn left to head East on Tunnel Hill Road. Drive for approximately 7 miles until you reach US-45.

Turn left onto US-45 to head North. Continue on US-45 for 4 miles until you reach Ozark Road. Then refer to the section below.

DIRECTIONS TO OZARK, IL FROM THE SOUTH

Make your way to I-24 and take I-24 West. Continue West along I-24 and take Exit 14 for US-45 toward Vienna.

At the intersection, turn right to head North on US-45. Drive for approximately 10 miles until you reach Ozark Road and then refer to the section below.

DIRECTIONS TO OZARK, IL FROM THE EAST, NORTHEAST

Make your way to I-64 and take I-64 West. Continue West along I-24 and take Exit 130 for IL-1 and US-45 toward Garyville.

Drive South on US-45 for roughly 60 miles until you reach Ozark Road. Then refer to the section below.

FROM OZARK, IL

Turn onto Ozark Road and continue on Ozark Road for 4.5 miles. The turn for Ozark Road is located directly across the street from The Ozark General Store. (See Image 1.)

Ozark Road intersects with Trigg Tower Road (County Road 8) near the Zion Church and Cemetery. Turn left onto Trigg Tower Road and drive until you see the sign pictured above (Image 2.)

Turn right onto Glen Street Falls Road (this is a gravel road - AWD is recommended.) Continue on Glen Street Falls Road until you reach the creek crossing. At the creek, turn right to park in the main lot or cross the creek to continue to the Dog Walk (see p. 31 for directions on descending into the canyon.)

Photo Jason Kehl Collection.

Photo Yusuf Daneshyar.

MANAGING RISK

It's likely that you've heard the phrase, "Climbing is a sport with inherent risks." An objectively accurate statement, this phrase serves as a reminder that, in climbing, there are certain variables that define personal safety. Being aware of and understanding how to manage these risks is a crucial component of your overall experience as a climber.

Personal safety in climbing is not an odds game like roulette. Accidents don't "just happen" randomly. More often than not, accidents are the result of inexperience, negligence and even pride. It's important to remember that you have the opportunity to assess risk beforehand. Not only that, you can use this risk assessment to inform your decisions as to how you should proceed. In this sense, climbing is much more like poker than roulette.

A professional card player understands the risks inherent in gambling, but develops and utilizes certain strategies to tip the odds in his or her favor. As a climber, you should do the same.

Stack the proverbial deck in your favor. In other words, take the time to address potential hazards and identify favorable solutions before you leave the ground. This exercise has the potential to eliminate most of the risk immediately- effectively securing your chances of playing a winning hand.

Knowing when to fold is equally important. Experienced card players are able to determine when their hand has missed and are willing to fold in order to avoid incurring further losses. In climbing, know when you lack the experience or knowledge to take on a particular challenge. Check your pride at the door and make good decisions.

While stacking the deck is impossible to do at the casino, it is not impossible to do at the cliff.

Know your closest extraction point.

Make sure your cell phone is charged before visiting the area.

Pack a spare key to your car and tell your partner where it is kept.

Be aware of potential hazards along the trail.

Always stick clip the fist bolt and inspect the hardware you are climbing on.

Always use a fireman's belay when rappelling.

Knowing the best way in and out of the canyon is critical in an emergency situation. In the event of an accident, you may need to guide emergency responders.

Your cellular phone is the best tool in an emergency situation. Make sure the battery is charged (keeping your phone in "airplane" mode will conserve its battery) and do not lock your phone with a passcode. Your partner or another individual may need access to your phone in case of an emergency.

In an emergency situation, you or your partner may need to leave the canyon to find cell reception or help. Keeping a spare key with your car ensures that the driver can access your vehicle in an emergency situation.

Parts of the upper trail cross streams that feed the many waterfalls in the canyon. Exercise caution when crossing near the crest of these waterfalls. It is easy to slip on rocks or lose your balance in the water. In the warmer months, be aware of poison ivy, copperheads, and ticks.

In some instances, the first bolt may be quite high or the climbing leading up to the first bolt may not be secure. Stick clipping is an effective way to ensure that you reach the first bolt without the risk of hitting the ground. Do not climb on equipment that appears damaged, rusty or heavily worn.

Rappelling is a risky activity with where the greatest potential for serious injury exists. Double check your system and have your partner back you up by providing a fireman's belay.

RESPONSIBLE USAGE

We are incredibly fortunate that climbing is admissible in this part of the Shawnee National Forest. It is important that we enjoy areas like Jackson Falls responsibly. These places are sensitive and our presence has a lasting impact on the ecology of the area. It is equally important to remember that Jackson Falls is a shared resource. The manner in which we conduct ourselves in a shared environment does affect others. Please keep the following in mind during your visit to Jackson Falls.

Camping in approved areas and adhering to established trails are simple ways to reduce potentially disastrous, long-term environmental damage. When climbing, consolidate your belongings by keeping your equipment nearby and off the trail. Spreading out and scattering equipment magnifies our footprint significantly by trampling vegetation, exacerbating soil erosion, and widening foot trails. As always, pack out what you carry in, but also make it a point to collect any litter you encounter during your visit.

Make sure to only use the existing parking lot or pull-offs along the road. Parking in the middle of the road or obstructing other vehicles to pass is not acceptable. In an emergency situation, rescue crews, firefighters, and paramedics will need access to this road. This road leads to the helicopter-landing pad and must remain clear for first responders. Blocking this road prevents professionals from doing their job and interferes with their ability to provide immediate care to an injured person.

If you choose to bring your dog, be sure to keep it on a leash. Many owners think their dog is well behaved and obedient, but please understand that others may not share the same sentiment. Allowing your pets to bark loudly or to run around in areas of high traffic can create potentially dangerous situations for others. These situations have the potential to distract the belayer and put his or her climber at risk.

Finally, I would like to stress that as a climber, you are a representative of your sport. We are not the only user group in this area nor do we have priority over other users. Hikers, equestrians, photographers, and naturalists deserve to enjoy this place just as much as we do. They are equally passionate about exploring Jackson Falls.

The way in which you interact with these individuals, as well as representatives of the Forest Service, will influence how climbers, as a user group, are perceived. It is important that we remain in good standing with other members of the community. In summary, to borrow a phrase from my friend Ray, "your behavior will help determine whether we retain the privilege to climb on these cliffs in the future" (Ray Ellington p. 30; Red River Gorge Rock Climbs 2nd Ed.)

Being considerate is not difficult, so I invite you to set an example and enjoy this area responsibly.

Photo left Amanda "Danger" Smith.

DISPERSED CAMPING

Camping is permissible in the existing sites found along the gravel road that leads to the Dog Walk. These sites are primitive and visitors are responsible for disposing of your own waste (refuse, human, or otherwise) responsibly. There is no running water and only one pit toilet has been installed at the main parking lot. Primitive camping requires users to be far more conscientious and hopefully encourages a greater sense of accountability.

While you may see others camping in the main parking lot and the clearing across the road, please note that camping within 100 feet of any water source is a strict violation of the Leave No Trace guidelines outlined by the United States Department of Agriculture's Forest Service. Vegetation near water is especially fragile. Running water often carries and deposits user created waste throughout the forest. Avoid source contamination by choosing an environmentally friendly campsite.

Camping in the canyon itself is strictly prohibited. Please understand that campsites have a considerable impact on the environment. They contribute to soil compaction & erosion and disrupt indigenous vegetative growth. That being said, please camp in the existing sites.

Be aware that during dry seasons there is a heightened risk of forest fires. For this reason, please respect any ban on campfires that the Forest Service may put into effect. Alerts and notices are generally passed along through word of mouth, but if you have any questions please contact the US Forest Service or visit their website for updated information.

Main Office (General Inquiries) 618-253-7114

Website (USFS Resources) http://www.fs.usda.gov/shawnee

AMENITIES

Marion is the closest town that offers opportunities to dine out, shop for groceries & supplies and connect to the internet. The town of Carbondale is further North and has the only rock climbing & camping outfitter in the area. Below are recommended places for individuals planning an extended trip to Jackson Falls.

GROCERY STORES	HOURS	APPROX. DIST.
Ozark General Store		
11935 U.S. 45	6:00 a.m. - 6:00 p.m	20 Minutes
Ozark, IL 62972		
Walmart Supercenter		
2802 Outer Dr, Marion, IL	Open 24 Hours	45 Minutes
(618) 997-5618		
Kroger		
1704 W Deyoung St, Marion, IL	Open 24 Hours	45 Minutes
(618) 993-6330		

WIRELESS INTERNET		
Panera Bread		
2704 W Deyoung St	6:00 a.m. - 10:00 p.m	45 Minutes
Marion, IL 62959		
(618) 993-2240		
Starbucks Coffee		
1704 W Deyoung St	6:00 a.m. - 7:00 p.m	45 Minutes
Marion, IL 62959		
(618) 993-6330		

OUTDOOR SUPPLIES		
Shawnee Trails Wilderness		
222 W Freeman St	10:00 a.m. - 6:00 p.m	1 Hour
Carbondale, IL 62901		

Photo Keving Todd

JOIN NOW...
AND PROTECT WHAT'S HOLY!

ica
Illinois Climbers Association

Dan Groves has his eye on the prize, the purchase of the Holy Boulders! 'Full Grain' V3

LEAVE NO TRACE PRACTICES

PACK IN, PACK OUT

There are no waste receptacles or trash removal services in the parking lot, camping areas, or in the canyon itself. As a result, waste management is our responsibility. Anything brought in with you during your visit should be taken out upon your departure. Please consider the following when visiting Jackson Falls:

1. Repackage food prior to your trip as a way to minimize the waste brought into natural areas.

2. Bring trash bags or plastic bins so that you can collect trash during your visit.

3. Take the time to look for trash, hygiene products and spilled food at your campsite before leaving.

DISPERSED CAMPING

There are no designated campsites at Jackson Falls, but there are a number of improvised sites that have been established by users over time. When camping, keep in mind that dispersed camping is only admissible at the top of the canyon. Camping in the canyon is strictly prohibited.

Dispersed camping is the term used for camping anywhere in the National Forest outside of a designated campground. Dispersed camping requires additional skills and knowledge that are necessary for camping responsibly. (Dispersed camping areas do not have the amenities of a campground such as trash removal, tables, fire pits, etc. and often do not have facilities.)

When washing dishes, carry water 200 feet away from streams and lakes. Using biodegradable soaps helps reduce water and soil contamination.

For more information, please consult the camping section on p. 14.

CAMPFIRES

Campfires create lasting impacts in sensitive areas like Jackson Falls. For that reason, it is important to comply with the following guidelines:

1. Campfires are prohibited in the canyon and during periods of time during which the Forest Service has issued a ban.

2. Campfires in the dispersed camping areas are permissible, but use fire rings that have been established through regular use. This will keep fires contained and limit scarring.

3. Keep fires small; only use sticks that can be broken by hand.

4. Campfires should never be left unattended. Put out campfires completely and scatter coals and ashes. Use water to cool the ashes.

HUMAN WASTE DISPOSAL

A pit toilet is located in the main parking lot and receives regular service and maintenance. Please refrain from throwing trash and non-biodegradable objects into the pit toilet. These objects must be removed, as they will not decompose. Often when sanitation workers remove these objects, they scatter them in the woods behind the pit toilet making it someone else's responsibility to collect.

Should you find yourself in need of the restroom but are not in proximity to the pit toilet, follow the guidelines listed below:

1. Human waste should be deposited in cat holes dug 6 to 8 inches.

2. When using improvised facilities, be sure to stay at least 200 feet from water, campsites, and trails.

3. Do not bury non-biodegradable products.

4. Cover and disguise the cat hole when finished.

FOREST SERVICE GUIDELINES

The Shawnee National Forest, of which Jackson Falls is a part, encompasses the Ozark and Shawnee Hills of Southern Illinois. The Shawnee (approximately 280,000 acres of forest) has been federally managed since its designation as National Forest in 1939 as part of Franklin D. Roosevelt's expansion of the National Parks System.

Although the Forest Service is chiefly responsible for maintaining and improving areas like Jackson Falls, we (as users) are equally responsible for protecting these resources by exploring them contentiously.

The Forest Service has established certain guidelines and regulations to keep us safe and to keep the natural resources scenic and unspoiled for other visitors. Following these guidelines is our opportunity to show our appreciation for both the efforts of the Forest Service and the area itself.

Also included in this section is the Forest Service's official position on recreational usage in the Shawnee. Again, this property is owned and managed by the Federal Government. In order to stay in good standing with land management and ensure ongoing usage for future generations, we must consider these guidelines when exploring the outdoors.

CONTACTS:

Shawnee National Forest Headquarters
50 Highway 45 South
Harrisburg, IL 62946
(618) 253 - 1060
mailroom_r9_shawnee@fs.fed.us

Hidden Springs Ranger District
602 North First Street
Route 45 North
Vienna, IL 62995
(618) 658 - 2111

OFFICIAL SHAWNEE NATIONAL FOREST POLICIES: RECREATIONAL USE

1. ROCK CLIMBING AND RAPPELLING ARE NOT PERMITTED IN NATURAL AREAS AS DESIGNATED BY THE FOREST SERVICE.

A Natural Area is any tract of land or water that supports unique examples of terrestrial or aquatic ecosystems, habitats and populations. The Shawnee National Forest has limited opportunities for rock climbing and rappelling in order to protect these fragile ecosystems and prevent soil compaction and erosion.

Check out p. 261 to see a list of designated Natural Areas in the Shawnee. Please be familiar with these areas and contact the Forest Service should you encounter an area whose status as a Natural Area is unclear to you.

Not knowing an area's designation as a Natural Area does not excuse violation of the restriction against climbing in a Natural Area; as climbers we are responsible for knowing which areas are open to climbing.

2. BOLTING AND ANCHOR REPLACEMENT MUST BE APPROVED BY THE FOREST SERVICE. CLIMBERS SHOULD ONLY USE EXISTING ANCHORS OR REMOVABLE PROTECTION WHEN CLIMBING IN RECREATIONAL AREAS.

Bolting, from the perspective of the Forest Service, has always been and continues to be an illegal activity that constitutes environmental devastation. Bolting that occurred prior to the Forest Service's knowledge of climbers as a user group was overlooked and exempt from this regulation. The Forest Service will permit bolted protection or anchor replacement only with the sole approval of the District Ranger.

Any individual who wishes to establish a route or retrofit an existing route for the purposes of recreational climbing by installing permanent bolts should first contact the District Ranger's office.

Jackson Falls is on the Hidden Springs Ranger District and should be contacted regarding this particular issue. Contact information for the Shawnee National Forest Headquarters has also been included should you have general inquiries about recreational usage in the Shawnee.

100% PERFORMANCE
100% COMFORT
0% COMPROMISE

TENAYA

OASI

SEASONS

Arguably the best time to visit Jackson Falls is between the months of September and December. Average temperatures range from 50 to 70 degrees Fahrenheit between sun up and sun down. Not only is the warm weather more agreeable, but the lack of humidity and low risk of precipitation makes the Fall a reasonably predictable season. The Spring (late March to late May) is equally enjoyable, however the chance of precipitation is much higher. As a result, certain areas may stay damp and un-climbable for several days. If you plan to visit after it has rained, choose to climb on the free standing blocks in the canyon like Spleef Peak, Lovely Tower, Mr. Jimmy Boulder or Railroad Rock. These blocks have very little vegetative growth on top and as a result they retain less moisture. For that reason, these areas tend to dry out faster than others.

The Winter can be enjoyable as long as your schedule is flexible. While temperatures generally do fall below freezing between December and February, it is not uncommon in the Midwest to encounter the unexpected 50 degree and sunny day. For the most part, it is not advised to climb during the winter due to the extreme cold. The lack of sunshine this time of year makes it even more difficult to stay warm. If you choose to climb during the winter, do so at the Promised Land as it sees direct sun most of the day.

While climbing is an option during the summer months, it is strongly discouraged. Extreme heat, humidity, poison ivy and insects make climbing during this time of year a fool's errand. Unlike the Western states, climbing in the shade will offer little relief. Humidity is the single most important climatological factor to consider when visiting Jackson Falls. Many of the climbs in this area rely on friction to make certain features usable. Conditions can make your project go without a hitch, or it can turn into an epic battle for the summit. If you're desperate to sample some of the country's best sandstone during the summer months, areas like Railroad Rock, Battle Axe Tower, and Hidden Peaks will offer relief from the sun as they each have narrow corridors that do not allow much natural light to enter. Be advised that climbing in the shade will protect you from the sun, but it will do no good against the humidity.

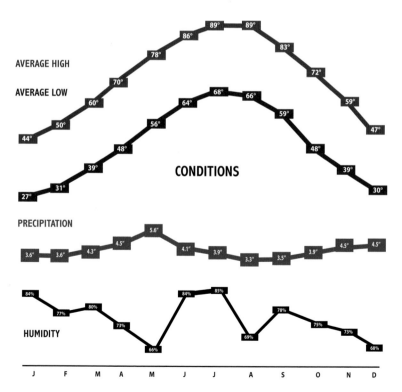

NATURAL HISTORY
BY PAUL HIME

Southern Illinois is a very special place. Most of the best climbing areas lie in the Shawnee Hills ecoregion, a habitat type characterized by abundant cliffs, canyons, and boulder fields interspersed across an oak-hickory forest. Together, Jackson Falls, Jackson Hollow and the Promised Land represent some of the best-of-the-best of Southern Illinois natural heritage, from exceptional climbing and bouldering to a rich and relatively intact natural experience.

The present day topology and character of Jackson Falls have been shaped over eons by the forces of plate tectonics and glaciation and more recently by the influences of human beings. The sandstone escarpments that dominate this region are ancient, having formed as marine sediments deposited on a seafloor in the Devonian period over 300 million years ago. As creeks cut through these layers of rock and as glaciers scoured this region time and time again, erosion and weathering exposed large sections of this tight-grained sandstone, some of the hardest on the continent. It can be humbling to think that one is literally climbing through ancient history along these routes, and in places the starting holds of a route may be tens of millions of years older than the finishing holds. Although these cliffs appear at first glance to be immutable and ageless, they are in fact dynamic entities, constantly changing. The features of the rock that we exploit today as handholds, smears, and tricam placements, as well the bolts and chains we install along the way, are only a tiny snapshot in the ever-changing existence of these precipices over geological time. Nonetheless, it is important for us to act as stewards of these magnificent walls and boulders and to ensure that future generations will be able to experience the wonder and beauty of this region.

The Jackson Falls area boasts an impressive array of species and it is this rich tapestry of life that sets such a perfect backdrop to climbing at these crags.

There can be large differences in the microclimate on top of and beneath the cliffs and the areas in canyons have acted as refugia for many relict species that occur in this area.

Photo Dan Brya...

JACKSON FALLS DISCOVERED

FFA OF BOLTED ONE 5.11D

MIKE SIMPSON AUTHORS FIRST JACKSON FALLS GUIDEBOOK

5.13 ESTABLISHED

CLIMBING RECOGNIZED BY THE FOREST SERVICE

VERTICAL HEARTLAND 1ST EDIT PUBLISHED BY ERIC ULNER

1981   1986   1989 1990 1991   1993

CLIMBING HISTORY

The potential for climbing at Jackson Falls was first discovered by Eric Ulner in 1981. While hiking at the nearby Jackson Hollow, Ulner came across a faint trail that led to what we now call the Northern Falls.

During the first few years of exploration, the canyon was combed exclusively for its naturally protectable lines. Spearheaded by Ulner, a small group of local climbers (including Jim Thurmond, Alan Carrier, and John Payne) established Squirrel House Crack 5.9, Applejack Crack 5.11b, and Deception 5.9. By the mid-1980s, many of the canyon's naturally protectable lines had been climbed. It was clear, however, that the canyon still offered more potential for climbing if its sheer faces were protectable.

Sport climbing at Jackson Falls matured at a time when the sport was changing. In the mid-1980s, the acceptance of permanent protection allowed climbers to explore opportunities that traditionally protected routes could not offer. The sport-climbing boom came to a head in the early 1990s when climbing potential in the Daniel Boone National Forest (Eastern Kentucky) was first discovered. The steep and pocketed nature of Kentucky sandstone was wildly different than anything people had seen before, and there was limitless first ascent potential. As a result, climbers began migrating east to explore the opportunities the Red River Gorge had to offer.

Despite this shift, individuals like Ulner, Payne, Carrier, and Thurmond remained in Illinois and bolted the first sport climbs in the canyon including Mary's Cookies 5.11d, Viking Blood 5.12c, and The Garden Route 5.10a. Unique to the area was its high concentration of climbs in the grade of 5.12. At the time, very few routes of that grade existed in the United States. For a place in the most unassuming part of the country to produce that many 5.12s was unheard of.

The first guidebook to catalog the growing number of sport routes in Jackson Falls was published in 1989. Authored and illustrated by Michael Simpson, the first-edition included roughly 50 routes between Railroad Rock and Spleef Peak. Two subsequent editions documented the rapid and ongoing development throughout the canyon.

Over time, word of the canyon's sport climbing potential began to spread throughout the region. For

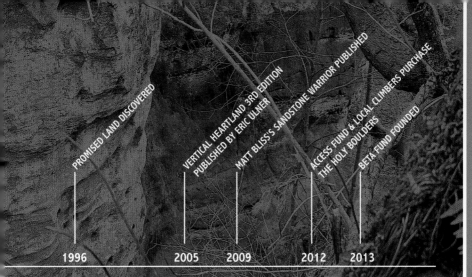

PROMISED LAND DISCOVERED

VERTICAL HEARTLAND 3RD EDITION PUBLISHED BY ERIC ULNER

MATT BLISS'S SANDSTONE WARRIOR PUBLISHED

ACCESS FUND & LOCAL CLIMBERS PURCHASE THE HOLY BOULDERS

BETA FUND FOUNDED

1996   2005   2009   2012   2013

climbers in the Midwest whose climbing resources were limited, Jackson Falls became an increasingly popular destination. In 1990, a set of Wisconsin climbers began mining the Falls for hard first ascents. During their initial visits, Rich Bechler and David Groth brought the grade of 5.13 to Jackson Falls by establishing routes like Butcher of Baghdad 5.13a, Emperor of the North 5.13a, and East of East St. Louis 5.13c. By 1990, roughly 100 routes had been bolted in the canyon. Jackson Falls was on the map and serving climbers from Wisconsin, Iowa, Missouri, Illinois, Indiana, and parts of the Southeast.

In response to growing recreational use at Jackson Falls and the risk of losing access to other local climbing areas like Cedar Bluff, Eric Ulner and John Payne (among others) formed the region's first local climber's organization. The Southern Illinois Climbers Alliance was established in 1991. The SICA, with help from the Access Fund, succeeded in including climbing as a recreational activity in the Forest Service's land management plan. Additionally, the climber-driven organization improved the parking lot at Jackson Falls by spreading gravel and installing the original information kiosk.

Eventually, other motivated individuals like Chris Schmick, Russell Rowlands, and Greg Thomas began exploring the canyon as well. In 1996, Schmick and Rowlands pursued opportunities beyond the main canyon. Their efforts yielded the discovery of an entirely new area on the other side of the railroad tracks - The Promised Land. In the early 2000s, local climber Jeff Frizzell moved back to Illinois after bolting routes in the burgeoning sport climbing scene in Smith Rock, Oregon. Using this newly acquired lens, Frizzell discovered some of the last gems in the canyon: Thrill Jill 5.12b, Little Johnny Jewel 5.11b, and King Snake 5.12d, among others.

Route development has continued off and on for the past two decades. Regional interest, on the other hand, continues to grow rapidly. The expansion of the climbing industry, the development of indoor climbing gyms and the advent of the Internet have produced more climbers and have helped spread information about the sport faster than ever before. Jackson Falls continues to be a premier climbing destination for the Midwestern States as well as the rest of the country.

(For a comprehensive history of climbing in Southern Illinois, refer to Eric Ulner's Vertical Heartland.)

p. 87. Jesse Koerner on Bursting Out 5.12C. Photo Jesse Koerner Collection.

BOULDERING

While Jackson Falls is primarily a sport climbing destination, there are a handful of quality boulders in the canyon as well. During colder months, when climbing on a rope can be unbearable, climbers in the area often explore the canyon for its bouldering resources.

Unlike other dedicated bouldering destinations, Jackson Falls does not have a high concentration of problems. That being said, the bouldering that is available is excellent. There are several areas in the surrounding region that can provide more opportunities for those looking to plan a bouldering trip. Areas like the Holy Boulders, the Beach, and the Roost are all within driving distance from Jackson Falls.

Individuals looking for more information should consult Matt Bliss's Sandstone Warrior. This is an excellent compilation that catalogues Southern Illinois' rich bouldering resources.

RECOMMENDED ROUTES

5.6
- [ ] BIG WALL GREG'S CHICKEN SHACK P. 68

5.7
- [ ] TINA'S SOUL FOOD KITCHEN P. 154

5.8
- [ ] MOD SQUAD P. 60
- [ ] LUSCIOUS BABES P. 72
- [ ] BLUE SPARK P. 128
- [ ] DEETLE DUMPS P. 152
- [ ] STUBBORN SWEDE P. 184

5.9
- [ ] THROUGH THE SMOKE P. 131
- [ ] FINE NINE P. 136
- [ ] THE MEANEST FLOWER P. 153
- [ ] GROOVY MARCIA P. 209

5.10A
- [ ] VENOM P. 70
- [ ] EARTHBOUND MISFIT P. 107
- [ ] ARCHANGEL P. 153
- [ ] CHEERIO BOWL P. 181
- [ ] KILL BILL P. 211

5.10B
- [ ] ALASKA P. 52
- [ ] SPIDERS FROM MARS P. 70
- [ ] WHO LET THE SNAKES OUT P. 144
- [ ] CUT THROAT P. 107
- [ ] THREE HOUR TOUR P. 198
- [ ] XOXO P. 230

5.10C
- [ ] TONS OF FUN P. 82
- [ ] GROUP THERAPY P. 106
- [ ] SORE THROAT P. 107

5.10D
- [ ] FRAGILE EGOS P. 37
- [ ] FLINGIN' HOG P. 60

5.11A
- [ ] WILD AT HEART P. 38
- [ ] WISHBONE P. 52
- [ ] LOVELY ARÊTE P. 138
- [ ] LASSO THE VULTURE P. 209
- [ ] FASHIONABLY LATE P. 246

5.11B
- [ ] THE DRIFTER P. 39
- [ ] STAND AND DELIVER P. 114
- [ ] GENERATOR X P. 230

5.11C
- [ ] BLUE VELVET P. 38
- [ ] MR. ALLISON'S COOKIES P. 53
- [ ] AUTOMATIC DAMNATION P. 170

5.11D
- [ ] AMERICAN HANDGUNNER P. 38
- [ ] MARY'S COOKIES P. 53
- [ ] STINGER P. 71
- [ ] THE BOLTED ONE P. 83
- [ ] THE VOW P. 153
- [ ] TACO'S ATV JAMBOREE P. 233

5.12A
- [ ] RAGING INTENSITY P. 48
- [ ] THE RECKONING P. 91
- [ ] HIDDEN TREASURE P. 138
- [ ] DETOX MOUNTAIN P. 178
- [ ] EVER READY BETTY P. 204
- [ ] TEAM HONDA P. 247

5.12B
- [ ] BARBARIANS AT THE GATE P. 36
- [ ] FRIZZLE FRY P. 63
- [ ] CRO-MAGNON WARRIOR P. 124
- [ ] SPACE COWBOY P. 199
- [ ] REMOVE LA ROPA P. 238

5.12C
- [ ] VIKING BLOOD P. 88
- [ ] LOST INNOCENCE P. 141
- [ ] HERE COME THE SNAKES P. 145
- [ ] DISCO FEVER P. 208
- [ ] BALANCE OF POWER P. 238

5.12D
- [ ] WORKING CLASS P. 50
- [ ] DSB P. 79
- [ ] KING SNAKE P. 83
- [ ] EMINENT DOMAIN P. 88
- [ ] INNER PIT BULL P. 148
- [ ] HUBBA HUBBA P. 234

5.13A
- [ ] BUTCHER OF BAGDAD P. 41
- [ ] MANUFACTURING CONSENT P. 50
- [ ] RED CORVETTE P. 61
- [ ] SHORTY THE PIMP P. 62
- [ ] EMPEROR OF THE NORTH P. 79

5.13B
- [ ] ZEN ARCADE P. 50
- [ ] LEGENDS OF THE FALLS P. 60
- [ ] POOL OF REFLECTION P. 234

5.13C
- [ ] EAST OF EAST ST. LOUIS P. 86

5.13D
- [ ] DYNASTY P. 79

JACKSON FALLS OVERVIEW

NORTHERN ACCESS

P
MAIN PARKING

RAILROAD ROCK

NORTH FALLS

Little Bay Creek

Glen Street Falls Road

HOBO CAVE

NORTH CANYON

MAIN POOL

WIZARD WALL

APPLEJACK

SPLEEF PEAK

THE DOORS

BATTLE AXE

BLACK SHEEP

GALLERY

WEST FALLS

LOVELY TOWER

BIG STAR WALL

DYNASTY WALL

ROYAL ARCHES

BEAVER WALL

RAINY DAY ROOF

MR. JIMMY

MANKY ALCOVE

INDUSTRY WALL

EAST FALLS

DOGWALK ACCESS

HIDDEN PEAKS

PROMISED LAND ←

DETOX

SOUTHERN ACCESS

BASEMENT

TOWN SQUARE

(H)

SOUTH CANYON

S.S. MINNOW

THE RANCH

4WD to Glen Street Falls Road

LA HACIENDA

GENTLEMENS GROTTO

JACKSON FALLS AREAS

RAILROAD ROCK

C. NORTHERN ACCESS

MAIN PARKING

P

NORTH CANYON
p. 32 – 73

NORTH FALLS
p. 112 – 155

Little Bay Creek

Glen Street Falls Road

HOBO CAVE

WEST FALLS
p. 74 – 111

GALLERY

SPLEEF PEAK

BATTLE AXE

LOVELY TOWER

BIG STAR WALL

DYNASTY WALL

BEAVER WALL

RAINY DAY ROOF

MR. JIMMY

INDUSTRY WALL

EAST FALLS
p. 156 – 165

A.

HIDDEN PEAKS

DOGWALK ACCESS

PROMISED LAND
p. 220 – 250

B. SOUTHERN ACCESS

TOWN SQUARE

S.S. MINNOW

SOUTH CANYON
p. 166 – 219

THE RANCH

APPROACH POINTS
A. DOG WALK ACCESS
B. SOUTHERN ACCESS
C. NORTHERN ACCESS

!!! USE EXTREME CAUTION WHEN CROSSING THE WATERFALLS !!!

30

Main Parking Lot - Before Driving over the First Creek

DESCENDING INTO THE CANYON

There are three descent options to consider when entering the canyon. Reference the map to locate the access points near Railroad Rock, the Dog Walk, and Hidden Peaks.

I strongly recommend using the Dog Walk to enter the canyon. Not only is the Dog Walk a relatively centralized point from which to start, it is arguably the safest and most responsible way to make your way to the valley floor.

DOGWALK ACCESS (A.)
FROM THE PARKING LOT (20 minutes)

Park in the main parking lot located on the right hand side of Glen Street Falls Road and prior to crossing Little Bay Creek (Photo 1.)

Hike downstream using the well-worn trail that parallels Little Bay Creek past the information kiosk. After hiking for approximately 5 minutes you will reach the edge of the cliff line. Turn left and follow the trail across the top of the cliff (Photo 2.) Exercise caution when crossing the first waterfall.

Crossing the North Falls. Dog Walk Access about 2700 feet.

After hiking approximately 15 minutes you will reach a second waterfall crossing (Photo 3.) Just beyond this crossing you will encounter a large boulder that caps a narrow hallway. This feature marks the natural staircase below known as the "Dog Walk" (Photo 4.)

FROM GLEN STREET FALLS ROAD (3 minutes)

From the main parking lot, hike or drive South for half a mile along the gravel road (Glen Street Falls Road.) If your vehicle has low clearance or does not have 4-wheel drive, it would be best to park in the main lot and either hike or find a ride.

Park on the right-hand side of the road using the existing pull-offs. Please keep in mind that parking is limited. Do your best to accommodate other visitors by parking close together.

The main trailhead itself is located on the West side of the road. A well-defined trail will lead you down hill toward the cliffline. After a short hike, the dirt foot trail will turn into a distinct sandstone path and will lead you to the stream that feeds the Eastern Waterfall.

Crossing the East Falls. Dogwalk Access is Behind Him.

After crossing the stream, continue hiking East along the trail that overlooks the canyon floor. Eventually you will encounter a large boulder that caps a narrow hallway. This feature marks the natural staircase below known as the "Dog Walk" (Photo 4.)

Once on the valley floor, head South through the narrow hallway to reach areas like Hidden Peaks and the Ranch. Otherwise, follow the cliffline North (the direction from which you came) to reach areas like Lovely Tower, the Gallery, Beaver Wall, and Railroad Rock.

SOUTHERN ACCESS (B.)

Begin your approach by parking in the main parking lot or along Glen Street Falls Road. Follow the corresponding directions to reach the Dog Walk Access.

After reaching the Dog Walk Access, hike approximately 700 yards South along the top trail. At this point, you will encounter the large, flaring ravine (See photo on p. 266.) This is the Southern access. Hike downhill through the ravine to reach the Hidden Peaks Area.

NORTHERN ACCESS (C.)

Park in the main lot and locate the well-worn trail that parallels Little Bay Creek.

Dogwalk Access. Approach is from top right of image.

Hike downstream along the trail past the information kiosk. This trail is designated as trail number 48. Markers indicating this designation will appear along the trail.

After roughly 700 yards, the trail will begin to descend down hill and cross near the crest of the West Waterfall. Exercise caution when crossing here. A brief hike up hill will put you back on the main trail.

From the trail you will see three large, freestanding boulders. The third boulder you will encounter is Railroad Rock. Once you have identified the Railroad Rock boulder, continue hiking along the trail for another 500 ft. You will see a small platform on your left; from this platform you will be able to descend down to the canyon floor. Once on the floor, hike back in the in the direction from which you came. A well-defined trail that follows the cliff line will take you back to Railroad Rock.

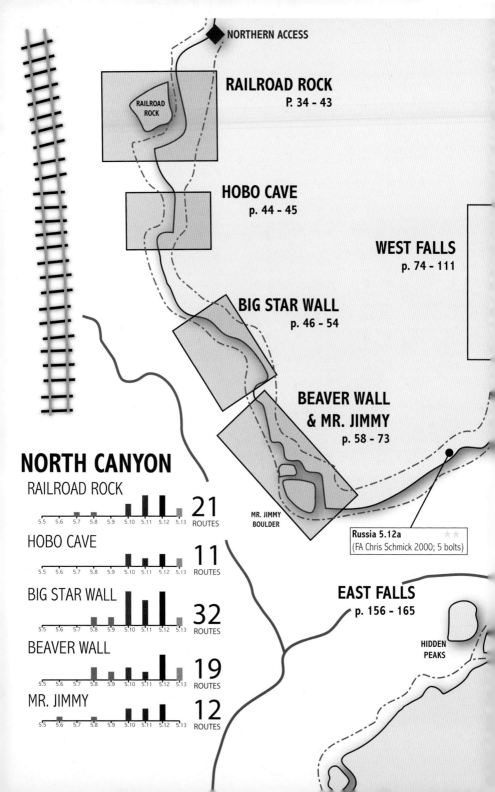

NORTHERN ACCESS

RAILROAD ROCK
P. 34 - 43

RAILROAD ROCK

HOBO CAVE
p. 44 - 45

WEST FALLS
p. 74 - 111

BIG STAR WALL
p. 46 - 54

BEAVER WALL & MR. JIMMY
p. 58 - 73

MR. JIMMY BOULDER

Russia 5.12a ★★
(FA Chris Schmick 2000; 5 bolts)

NORTH CANYON

RAILROAD ROCK

5.5 5.6 5.7 5.8 5.9 5.10 5.11 5.12 5.13
21 ROUTES

HOBO CAVE

5.5 5.6 5.7 5.8 5.9 5.10 5.11 5.12 5.13
11 ROUTES

BIG STAR WALL

5.5 5.6 5.7 5.8 5.9 5.10 5.11 5.12 5.13
32 ROUTES

BEAVER WALL

5.5 5.6 5.7 5.8 5.9 5.10 5.11 5.12 5.13
19 ROUTES

MR. JIMMY

5.5 5.6 5.7 5.8 5.9 5.10 5.11 5.12 5.13
12 ROUTES

EAST FALLS
p. 156 - 165

HIDDEN PEAKS

Eric Ulner

More than anyone, Eric Ulner has devoted his life to the development of climbing in Southern Illinois. Between the mid 1980s and late 1990s Eric established roughly 40 unique routes at Jackson Falls- many of which are considered by most to be five star lines. With few exceptions, the routes Eric authored nearly three decades ago continue to stand out as the most climbed and talked about routes in the canyon.

When Eric began his efforts in 1985, Jackson Falls, then referred to as "The Hollow Behind the [Jackson] Hollow," was unequivocally unexplored and untouched by climbers. In fact, much of the cliff we see today was, at that time, carpeted with a thick layer of moss and lichen. Entire blocks, including Battle Axe Tower and the Mr. Jimmy Boulder, were hidden, buried even, under the vegetation. Equipped with nothing more than a wire brush and a relentless desire to discover what lay beneath, Eric spent what little free time he had unearthing these hidden treasures.

Eric often jokes that his fifth year pursuing an undergraduate degree at Southern Illinois University Carbondale was the result of his time spent bolting in Jackson Falls, "I'm still paying for my time down there." The fruits of his labor, however, bore stunning classics like Venom 5.10b, The Vow 5.11d, and Viking Blood 5.12c.

Over the course of Jackson Fall's development, user created trails made accessing other parts of the canyon more manageable. These trails eventually allowed for route development to grow exponentially. The more accessible the cliff became, the more quickly routes went up. However, at the time of Eric's campaign, these trails (the ones we so often take for granted) had not yet been established, "If you wanted to walk past Group Therapy 5.10c, you had to fight your way through sticker bushes and poison ivy. It grew right up to the cliff."

Despite these challenges, ones that would dissuade even the most adventurous individual, Eric continued to work tirelessly to explore and document this new area.

In 1992, after spending nearly 20 years in the canyon, Eric compiled his notes in order to produce one of the first guides to climbing in Southern Illinois, Vertical Heartland. Seven months of Eric's life were dedicated to amending previous versions of the guide with a comprehensive climbing history. During this time, Eric took an unpaid leave of absence from work to ensure the completion of his third edition.

Without Eric Ulner's tireless devotion and dedication, we would not have the same opportunities to climb as we have today. Eric Ulner started a revolution that made climbing possible in Southern Illinois and, as a result, opened doors for us all. Eric Ulner, a person who so strongly represents the commitment and sacrifices it takes to make the impossible possible, is without question a man to whom we owe much gratitude.

Photos Top: Kevin Todd, Right: Dan Brayack.

NOTABLE
FIRST ASCENTS

p. 38. Jaime Kreft on Wild at Heart 5.11a. Photo Matthew P. Guempel.

BACK WALL
p. 42 - 43

AM

RAILROAD ROCK

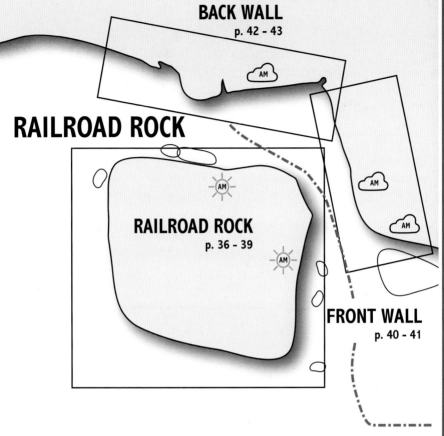

RAILROAD ROCK
p. 36 - 39

AM

AM

AM

AM

FRONT WALL
p. 40 - 41

RAILROAD ROCK

Railroad Rock is an exceptional area and has the highest concentration of five-star routes ranging from 5.10 to 5.13. This area stays shaded most of the day, making it a great place to climb if you want to avoid the heat.

Railroad Rock is also home to one of the canyon's best routes, **"WILD AT HEART" 5.11A.**

APPROACH
Use the Dog Walk to descend into the canyon. (A detailed description of this descent can be found on p. 31.)

Hike West along the main trail that follows the cliffline. Railroad Rock is located near the train tracks and just past the Hobo Cave.

The first routes you will encounter from this approach are on Railroad Rock, numbers 1-5.

RAILROAD ROCK

Routes 1 through 11 wrap around the Railroad Rock boulder and are number from left to right.

☐ **1. ELECTROCUTIONER**   **5.8**   ★★★

Located near the tracks, this route climbs through the questionable looking (but resilient) stone and can be identified by the large recess near the third bolt. This one may take some time to figure out.   (FA Jim Thurmond 1987; 6 bolts)

☐ **2. EGO TRIPPING**   **5.10A**   ★★★★

Stop reading this and tie in. Yeah, it really IS that good. What are you waiting for?! (FA Jeff Frizzell 2004; 7 bolts)

☐ **3. FRAGILE EGOS**   **5.10D**   ★★★★

See right.

☐ **4. BARBARIANS AT THE GATE 5.12B**   ★★★★

Serious pocket pulling down low gives way to fierce and unrelenting crimp climbing. Save some steel for the top. (FA Rich Bechler 1990; 7 bolts)

☐ **5. DAMN YANKEES**   **5.12C**   ★★★★

Attempt to climb the left side of this baffling arête. I have never made it past the first bolt, but the slab up there looks great! (FA Jim Thurmond 1990; 7 bolts)

☐ **3. FRAGILE EGOS   5.10D**
Begin by reaching between large sloping huecos and
pockets. Grab a shake at the ledge and finish by crimp-
ing your way up the superb face.
(FA Jane Sparboro 1981; 7 bolts)

Jaime Kreft going on Fragile Egos 5.10d. Photo Matthew P. Guempel.

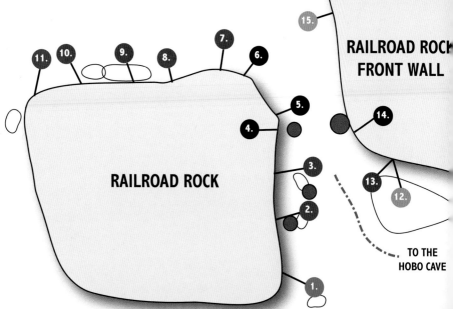

RAILROAD ROCK
FRONT WALL

RAILROAD ROCK

TO THE
HOBO CAVE

☐ **6. WHERE'S MY BOURBON 5.12B** ★★★★
Attempt to climb the right side of the same baffling
arête. (FA Dave Groth 1990; 6 bolts)

☐ **7. BLUE VELVET   5.11C** ★★★★★
A very challenging section down low on coarse
stone yields better rock quality above.
(FA Rich Bechler & Rob Drysdale 1992; 5 bolts)

☐ **8. WILD AT HEART   5.11A** ★★★★★
Without a doubt the perfect rock climb: breathtaking aesthetics, committing movement, and just
enough holds to make it possible. Start on the
large detached flake at the base of the cliff to
reach the starting holds. Pull on perfect pockets
to gain the large crescent feature that guards the
anchors. This is the best route at Jackson Falls and
is easily the best route I have done in my personal
climbing career. (FA Rich Bechler 1990; 5 bolts)

☐ **9. AMERICAN HANDGUNNER 5.11D** ★★★★
This thin and powerful face climb is one of Jackson
Falls' best-kept secrets.
(FA Rich Bechler 1990; 5 bolts)

10. THE DRIFTER 5.11B ★★★★

Another outstanding, unique line. Spectacular pocket pulling leads to a well-defined crux. Yard through slim holds to gain the chains.
(FA Rich Bechler 1991; 5 bolts)

11. ASTROLOGICAL SOUL TRAIN 5.10B ★★★

This route ascends the arête located on the right side of the Railroad Boulder. A challenging start with a precarious landing zone leads to more featured terrain above.
(FA Eric Ulner 1990; 5 bolts)

9.

10.

11.

RAILROAD ROCK FRONT WALL

Routes 12 through 15 climb the main cliffline next to and behind the Roadroad Rock Boulder. They are numbered from right to left.

☐ **12. ACCESS GRANTED 5.13A** ★★★
This route is on the main wall facing the train tracks and begins on the large block below. Unrepeated since Brad Weaver grabbed the first ascent back in 2007. This one looks rough! (FA Brad Weaver 2007; 4 bolts)

☐ **13. IN   5.11C** ★★
Around the right side of the arête on the cliff line is this dicey face climb. Make your way up the left slanting crack to gain the face and then head toward right-angling arête.
(FA Dave White & Dan Caldwell 1999; 3 bolts)

RAILROAD ROCK
p. 36 – 39

RAILROAD RO
FRONT WAL

TO
HOBO CAVE

14. PERMISSION DENIED 5.12B ★★

This face climb is located on the main cliffline, catty-corner from the Railroad Rock Boulder and between the tree and the arête near the outer portion of the corridor. (FA Chris Schmick 1992; 6 bolts)

15. BUTCHER OF BAGHDAD 5.13A ★★★★

This route is Jackson Fall's technical test piece and is the solitary weakness in the blood red section of sandstone on the main wall. You might want to wait for the right conditions; it's bleak up there. (FA Dave Groth 1990; 6 bolts)

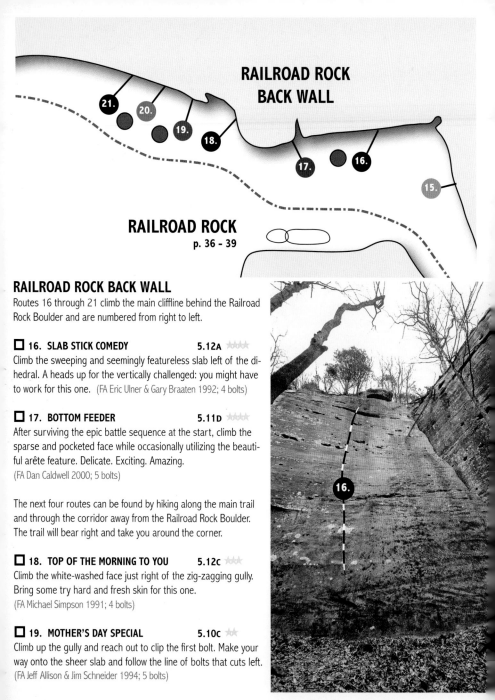

RAILROAD ROCK
p. 36 - 39

RAILROAD ROCK BACK WALL

Routes 16 through 21 climb the main cliffline behind the Railroad Rock Boulder and are numbered from right to left.

☐ **16. SLAB STICK COMEDY**　　　**5.12A** ★★★★

Climb the sweeping and seemingly featureless slab left of the dihedral. A heads up for the vertically challenged: you might have to work for this one.　(FA Eric Ulner & Gary Braaten 1992; 4 bolts)

☐ **17. BOTTOM FEEDER**　　　**5.11D** ★★★★

After surviving the epic battle sequence at the start, climb the sparse and pocketed face while occasionally utilizing the beautiful arête feature. Delicate. Exciting. Amazing.
(FA Dan Caldwell 2000; 5 bolts)

The next four routes can be found by hiking along the main trail and through the corridor away from the Railroad Rock Boulder. The trail will bear right and take you around the corner.

☐ **18. TOP OF THE MORNING TO YOU**　　　**5.12C** ★★★

Climb the white-washed face just right of the zig-zagging gully. Bring some try hard and fresh skin for this one.
(FA Michael Simpson 1991; 4 bolts)

☐ **19. MOTHER'S DAY SPECIAL**　　　**5.10C** ★★

Climb up the gully and reach out to clip the first bolt. Make your way onto the sheer slab and follow the line of bolts that cuts left.
(FA Jeff Allison & Jim Schneider 1994; 5 bolts)

20. PROCRASTINATION   5.7 ★★

Just left of the previous line is this heavily featured face climb. Pull on iron plates until you reach the anchors just above the small bulge at which point your patience will be put to the ultimate test. (FA Mike Killian 2002; 4 bolts)

21. CHEAP FAME   5.12A ★★★

This route will take you through the prominent dark streak on the left hand side of the wall prior to where the cliffline begins to break down.

(FA Jim Schneider & Margy Roth 1993; 4 bolts)

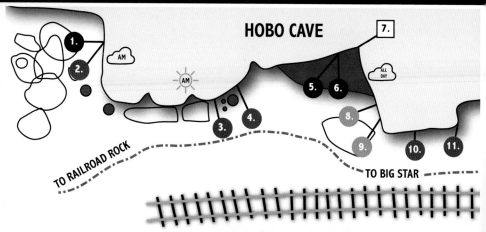

HOBO CAVE

1.

2.

AM

AM

3.

4.

5.

6.

7.

8.

9.

10.

11.

ALL DAY

TO RAILROAD ROCK

TO BIG STAR

HOBO CAVE

Hobo Cave is the impressive overhanging wall around the corner from the Big Star Wall. The routes in the cave itself start at 5.12a, but the main cliffline that leads back to Railroad Rock has more moderate climbs.

APPROACH

Use the Dog Walk to descend into the canyon. (A detailed description of this descent can be found on p. 31.)

Hike West along the main trail that follows the cliffline. The Hobo cave is located near the railroad tracks around the corner from the Big Star Wall.

The first route you will encounter from this approach is route number 11, **"PULL MY FINGER" 5.10D.**

☐ **1. THE BIG EASY**   **5.12B** ★★
Climb the sheer face using holds that gradually get thinner and thinner. At the fifth bolt, attempt to move leftward by making use of what few holds exist. (FA Eric Miller 2012; 6 bolts)

☐ **2. THE EASIER VARIATION**   **5.11D** ★★★
This route breaks right at the fifth bolt where **"BIG EASY"** moves left. Seriously sharp crimp climbing leads to the ledge below the small roof. Get it back here before attempting to negotiate the roof; this one is a total photo finish.
(FA Eric Miller 2012; 6 bolts)

David Quinney Living on the Edge 5.13a.   Photo Kevin Sierzega.

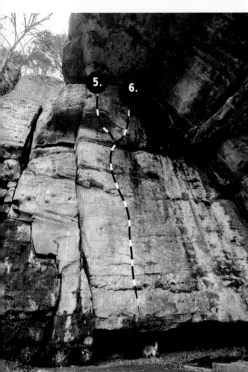

☐ **3. FLUFFY FLY**   **5.11c** ✦✦✦
Identifiable by the prominent water groove near the upper third of the cliff, this route climbs the tall face.
(FA Phillip Carrier and Jared Smith 2007; 7 bolts)

☐ **4. FRIGID DIGIT**   **5.10a** ✦✦✦
Long and varied, this route is a true adventure. Begin by climbing the pocketed slab to the right of the tree. Prepare for the change up at the 4th bolt and enjoy steep climbing on good holds to gain the face above.
(FA Mike Balossi, Darrell Sauer & Jeff Stockton 2003; 7 bolts)

☐ **5. BELCHING FIANCÉ**   **5.12a** ✦✦
Climb the vertical, ink-stained face beneath the large roof. Break left after the last bolt.
(FA Chris Schmick 1994; 6 bolts)

☐ **6. ANIMAL HUSBANDRY**   **5.12c** ✦
Climb **"BELCHING FIANCÉ"** and continue straight up through the relatively blank section of coarse stone. As you fight your way through savage terrain, take comfort in knowing that you're not the only one who wished they headed left at the last bolt.
(FA Greg Thomas 1994; 6 bolts)

☐ **7. LEFT TURN**   **A3/A1** ✦✦✦
This aid line follows the thin seam in the prominent dihedral feature. (FA Phil Patz & John Hein 2001; Gear)

☐ **8. CLOSER TO THE EDGE**   **5.13b** ✦✦✦
Moderate climbing gives way to a very difficult, but short-lived, crux. An incredible sport climb that may convince pad-people to put on a harness!
(FA Brian Capps 2014; 6 bolts)

☐ **9. LIVING ON THE EDGE**   **5.13a** ✦✦✦✦
This demanding face climb takes some serious try-hard. Tie in, step up and pull down on some of the best grips in the canyon.
(FA Greg Thomas & Chris Schmick 1994; 5 bolts)

☐ **10. Y TY N**   **5.10b** ✦✦
This is the first bolted route you will encounter around the corner from the large amphitheater. A quick hike up hill will lead you to this short and burly face climb. (FA Ron Hewitt 2001; 3 bolts)

☐ **11. PULL MY FINGER**   **5.10d** ✦✦
Climb the blunt, rust-striped arête.
(FA Ron Hewitt 2001; 4 bolts)

p. 50. Eric Widing on Manufacturing Consent 5.13a. Photo Kevin Sierzega.

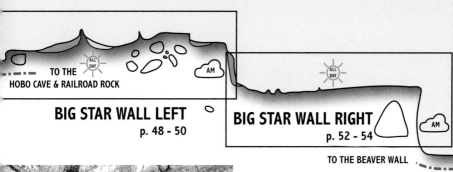

TO THE
HOBO CAVE & RAILROAD ROCK

BIG STAR WALL LEFT
p. 48 - 50

BIG STAR WALL RIGHT
p. 52 - 54

TO THE BEAVER WALL

BIG STAR WALL

As the name implies, the Big Star Wall is Jackson Falls' largest library of five-star routes. Expect technical climbing and exciting challenges. This is also one of the few areas that can accommodate a wide range of climbing abilities from 5.9 to 5.13.

Some of these climbs feature low cruxes, so be sure to stick clip the first bolt.

APPROACH

Use the Dog Walk to descend into the canyon. (A detailed description of this descent can be found on p. 31.)

Hike West along the main trail that follows the cliffline. The Big Star Wall is located around the corner from the Beaver Wall.

The first bolted route you will encounter is route number 32, **"CONSPIRACY THEORIST" 5.11B**.

Photo Elodie Saracco.

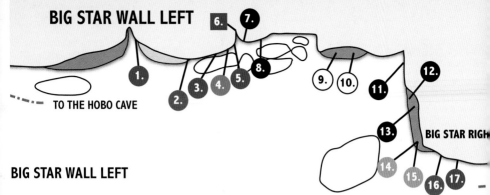

BIG STAR WALL LEFT

TO THE HOBO CAVE

BIG STAR RIGH

BIG STAR WALL LEFT

☐ **1. UNDEROOS FOR KANGAROOS 5.10A** ✫✫✫
This route can be tricky to find, but is well worth the hunt! Prior to the large, overhanging wall is a slabbier section of the cliff. Look for the small tree growing out of the cliff to spot the bolts. (FA Kipp Trummel 2004; 10 bolts)

☐ **2. REDUCTION** **5.11C** ✫✫
Step through the narrow corridor and make your way down hill to the platform provided by the small boulder at the base of the cliff. Walk to the left side of the boulder to reach the starting holds. Stick clip the first bolt before you take off! (FA Kipp Trummel 2004; 7 bolts)

☐ **3. TEAR STAINED EYE** **5.10B** ✫✫✫
Using the same approach to reach **"REDUCTION,"** make your way to the platform boulder. This is the first bolted route you will encounter and climbs through the prominent dark streak. (FA Jeff Frizzell & David Kessler 2004; 6 bolts)

☐ **4. TRAIN IN VAIN** **5.9** ✫✫✫
This route begins in the shallow dihedral and climbs the white face. (FA Mike Balossi & Jeff Stockton 2003; 6 bolts)

☐ **5. PITA** **5.10A** ✫✫✫
In the narrow chimney-like feature is this dark and impressive slab. (FA Ray Whaley 1996; 5 bolts)

☐ **6. NO PAYNES IN HEAVEN** **5.10C** ✫✫✫✫
Climb the crack to gain the striking dihedral feature. Take a breath and finish up by climbing the horizontal seam beneath the roof. (FA John Payne 1987; Gear)

☐ **7. RAGING INTENSITY** **5.12A** ✫✫✫✫
This route ascends the brilliant arête. Make your way to the anchors by sampling holds on both sides. (FA Greg Thomas 1991; 6 bolts)

☐ **8. MASON DIXON LINE** 5.12c ★★★
This route climbs through the oblong hueco in the middle of the face. A unique and challenging crux down low gives way to another unique and challenging crux above. (FA Rich Bechler 1991; 6 bolts)

☐ **9. PROJECT**
Attempt to climb the impossible golden face. This route is not currently equipped with anchors. (5 bolts)

☐ **10. BLAZED OF GLORY PROJECT**
Attempt to climb the blood-red face left of the dihedral. This route does not have top anchors. It looks really bleak up there. (Equipped by Chris Loesch; 6 bolts)

☐ **11. JONES'N IN JACKSONVILLE** 5.12A ★★★
This is the first bolted sport climb to right of the dihedral. Come equipped with a strong crimp game and relentless tenacity if you want to tangle with this rig. Race through small edges to reach the stiff pocket crux near the top. Try to keep it together while negotiating the dihedral section above; you could definitely blow it there. (FA Scott Swanson & Thad Ferrell 1998; 7 bolts)

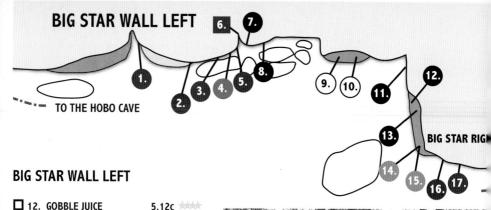

BIG STAR WALL LEFT

TO THE HOBO CAVE

BIG STAR RIGH

BIG STAR WALL LEFT

☐ **12. GOBBLE JUICE** 5.12c ★★★★
Not the most aesthetic route, but definitely a good ride. This route tackles the overhanging, detached flake. Turn the corner to gain the headwall and prepare yourself for the pump crux that guards the chains. (FA Chris Schmick & Greg Thomas 1994; 10 bolts)

☐ **13. WORKING CLASS** 5.12d ★★★★
This route can be identified by the eye-bolts at the start. Bigger and badder than the previous route, steep stone gives way to the thin, technical finish. (FA Dave Groth 1991; 10 bolts)

The next two routes share the first two bolts.

☐ **14. ZEN ARCADE** 5.13b ★★★★
Just left of the rounded arête is the start of this thin and demanding climb. This direct line heads straight up the face (staying straight at the second bolt.) Pull on poor holds to reach the break. Shake it off and bust through back-to-back cruxes. (FA Dave Groth 1993; 9 bolts)

☐ **15. MANUFACTURING CONSENT 5.13a** ★★★★
This route shares the start of **"ZEN ARCADE,"** but breaks right after the second bolt. Siege the steep and imposing face above. (FA Tom Ramie 1993; 8 bolts)

p. 52. Jaime Kreft on Express Checkout Line 5.9.   Photo Matthew P. Guempel.

BIG STAR WALL RIGHT

☐ 16. LADYBUG LYNN   5.11B ★★★★
Begin on **"EXPRESS CHECKOUT LINE"** to gain the ledge.
Traverse left until you reach the second line of bolts.
"LADYBUG LYNN" and **"ALASKA"** are squeezed together
between the two dark streaks. For clarification, this is the
left-most route. (FA Dan Smith & Shawn Watson 2000; 6 bolts)

☐ 17. ALASKA   5.10B ★★★★
Begin on **"EXPRESS CHECKOUT LINE"** to gain the ledge.
Traverse left until you encounter the first line of bolts in the
dark streak and head straight up.
(FA Dan Smith & Ron Hewitt 2000; 7 bolts)

☐ 18. EXPRESS CHECKOUT LINE 5.9 ★★★★
Begin by palming and smearing to gain the large ledge.
Climb through a variety of sloped and positive holds, mak-
ing use of the occasional jug to grab a quick shake. This
truly enjoyable climb shouldn't be overlooked!
(FA Eric Ulner 1992; 6 bolts)

☐ 19. COCOA RAE   5.10C ★★★
Make your way onto the large, dark ledge just left of the
two parallel water grooves that define the **"BIRTHDAY
ROUTE."** Be careful clipping the second bolt and head up
the dark streak. (FA Keith Adams & Dave Downey 1998; 6 bolts)

☐ 20. BIRTHDAY ROUTE   5.10B ★★★
This is the most recognizable route in the area. Find the
path of least resistance offered by the pillar feature.
(FA Eric Ulner & Kathy Ulner 1992; 7 bolts)

☐ 21. DA BRO   5.10B ★★★
Located directly right of the **"BIRTHDAY ROUTE"** pillar is this
baffler. Try A LOT harder than you expected to in order to
gain the face. (FA Mike Balossi & Jeff Stockton 2001; 8 bolts)

☐ 22. STINGRAY   5.10D ★★
Start just left of the 45 degree angling crack/seam which
crosses **"WISHBONE"** at about 20 feet. Clip the second
bolt and muster up the courage to leave the safety of the
ledge. Touching those holds ten more times won't make
them better; you're just going to have to stick and move!
(FA Jeff Frizzell & Bill Rodgers 2004; 8 bolts)

☐ 23. WISHBONE   5.11A ★★★★
A popular route among most climbers in the area and
one that is guaranteed to keep you on your toes! Begin
on the face in front of the beech tree (the initials "KB"
and "AB" are carved into the trunk.)
(FA Chris Schmick 2000; 9 bolts)

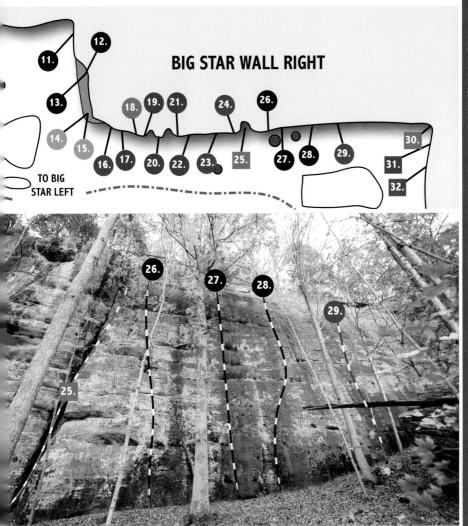

BIG STAR WALL RIGHT

TO BIG
STAR LEFT

☐ **24. MR. ALLISON'S COOKIES 5.11C**
This route ascends the light gray section of the wall
directly left of the large off-width climb, **"FREE DAY."**
(FA Jeff Allison & Jim Schneider 1999; 7 bolts)

☐ **25. FREE DAY 5.8**
This is the long and continuous crack that separates the
5.10 section of the wall from the 5.12 wall. An obvious
feature that begs to be climbed.
(FA Phil Patz & John Hein 2002; Gear)

☐ **26. SUN RA 5.12B**
Start 20 feet right of the **"FREE DAY"** crack on the
crack/seam just left of the tree. The route climbs the
technical and demanding slab.
(FA Jeff Frizzell 2004; 8 bolts)

☐ **27. BIG STAR 5.12B**
Start just right of the big tree. A surprisingly challenging start leads to easier, albeit delicate terrain. Don't
blow it! (FA Jeff Frizzell 2004; 8 bolts)

☐ **28. GALAXY 500 5.12A**
Tenuous pocket pulling leads to the brilliant and committing sequence on the faint right-angling seam. Get it
back at the third and keep it together; it's not over 'til
it's over. (FA Jeff Frizzell 2004; 8 bolts)

☐ **29. MARY'S COOKIES 5.11D**
Sporty, for sure. Insecure and committing in all the
wrong places. This line follows the left-angling seam.
Arguably the best line on the wall.
(FA John Payne 1987; 6 bolts)

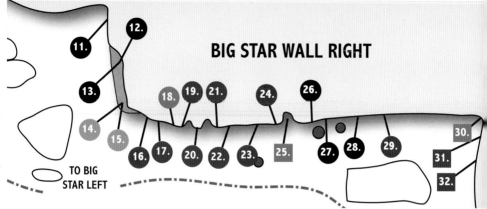

BIG STAR WALL RIGHT

TO BIG
STAR LEFT

☐ **30. CHIT CHAT** **5.8** ⭐⭐
This gear line takes the large dihedral on the right hand side of the Big Star Wall.
(FA Michael Simpson 1987; Gear)

☐ **31. GET OUT OF MY KITCHEN** **5.10c** ⭐
This route begins on the left-angling crack and climbs into **"CHIT CHAT."**
(FA Leif Faber 1991; Gear)

☐ **32. CONSPIRACY THEORISTS** **5.11b** ⭐
This is the only route with bolts on the wall. These bolts will need to be supplemented with some gear. (FA Chris Schmick 2001; 5 bolts + Gear)

belay
specs

Made in USA
www.belayspecs.com

p. 60. Chuck McGibbon on the bulgy Flingin' Hog 5.10d.   Photo Matthew P. Guempel.

p. 70. Yusuf Daneshyar on Spiders from Mars 5.10b.   Photo Dan Brayack.

p. 60. Eric Widing poised on Legends of the Falls 5.13b. Photo Jesse Koerner.

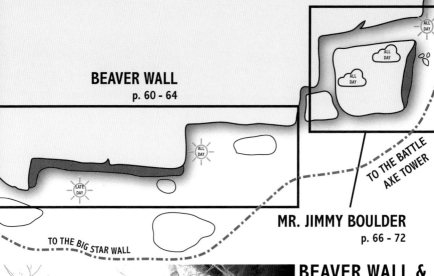

BEAVER WALL
p. 60 - 64

TO THE BATTLE
AXE TOWER

MR. JIMMY BOULDER
p. 66 - 72

TO THE BIG STAR WALL

ALL DAY

LATE DAY

BEAVER WALL & MR. JIMMY

The Beaver Wall offers the best steep climbing in the canyon. Don't be fooled by the height; you can definitely catch a pump here! Popular routes include **"FRIZZLE FRY" 5.12B** and **"WHO NEEDS FRIENDS" 5.12A.**

Mr. Jimmy is the freestanding boulder located just beyond the Beaver Wall. Proper slab climbing at its best: technical, committing and seemingly improbable. Take these routes over the top for an amazing view. Don't miss **"SPIDERS FROM MARS" 5.10B** and **"STINGER" 5.11D.**

APPROACH

Use the Dog Walk to descend into the canyon. (A detailed description of this descent can be found on p. 31.)

Hike West along the main trail that follows the cliffline. Beaver Wall and Mr. Jimmy are located around the corner from the Dynasty Wall.

The first bolted route you will encounter is route number 3, **"POINT BLANK" 5.11D** just before the Mr. Jimmy Boulder.

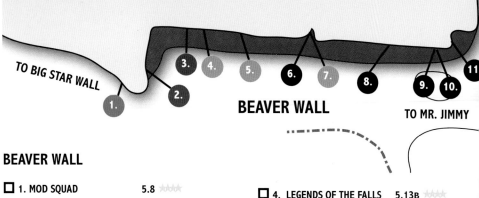

BEAVER WALL

☐ **1. MOD SQUAD**   **5.8** ★★★
This heavily featured slab faces the main trail as well as the large boulder on the opposite side of the trail. A good romp and an absolute must for those just starting their climbing experience.   (FA Unknown; 8 bolts)

☐ **2. FLINGIN' HOG**   **5.10D** ★★
Left of the dihedral is this gently overhanging face climb. Give it some gas to make it through the first few bolts, but tap the breaks for the technical challenge near the top!
(FA John & Maria Sommerhof, Geoff Thorsen, Kerby McGhee 1992; 7 bolts)

☐ **3. THE FALL OF LEGENDS**   **5.11c** ★★
Don't get ahead of yourself! This feel good ride comes to a grinding halt as you make a play for the anchors.
(FA Russell Errett 2013; 4 bolts)

☐ **4. LEGENDS OF THE FALLS**   **5.13B** ★★★
Moderately difficult climbing takes you to the harsh undercling crux. Stick and move!
(FA Brice Dion 1997; 4 bolts)

☐ **5. RED CORVETTE**   **5.13A** ★★★
See right.

☐ **6. WHO NEEDS FRIENDS?**   **5.12A** ★★★
This route is the left-angling crack in the center of the wall. Grovel through sandy stone to reach the no hands rest at the first bolt. Shake it off and hike through positive holds (and the occasional hand jam) to reach the anchors.
(FA Chris Schmick & Greg Thomas 1993; 6 bolts)

☐ **5. RED CORVETTE 5.13A**
This route can be identified by the lone hueco and the large iron knob near the first bolt. Exciting and varied, you'll earn all thirteen points if you can clip the chains on this one.
(FA Kurt Smith 1995; 5 bolts)

Jesse Koerner fights hard on the dynamic finish of Red Corvette 5.13a. Photo Kevin Sierzega.

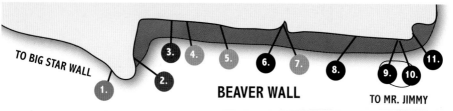

BEAVER WALL

TO BIG STAR WALL

TO MR. JIMMY

☐ **7. SHORTY THE PIMP** 5.13A ★★★
Begin by climbing the face just right of **"WHO NEEDS FRIENDS."** Race through good holds until they run out. Pull out all the stops to connect the dots in the short, but powerful crux above.
(FA Larry Harris 1995; 4 bolts)

☐ **8. FRIZZLE FRY** 5.12B ★★★★
See right.

☐ **9. EVERYBODY NEEDS FRIENDS** 5.12A ★★★★
Steep and varied climbing with a heartbreaker finish. Don't feel bad if you blow it at the end; we all have!
(FA Greg Thomas 1995; 4 bolts)

☐ **10. TASMANIAN DEVIL** 5.12B ★★★
Begin on **"EVERYBODY NEEDS FRIENDS"** and break right after clipping the first bolt. Despite being the original line, this one doesn't receive as much attention.
(FA Eric Ulner 1992; 4 bolts)

☐ **11. SPITS OR SWALLOWS** 5.12A ★★
Climb the face just right of the blunt arête. A tricky mantle protects the anchors.
(FA Phillip Carrier 2010; 4 bolts)

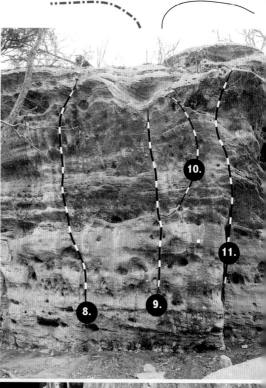

☐ **8. FRIZZLE FRY** **5.12B**

Hyper-classic! The pump builds fast on this one and you'll want some steam for the top. Punch it between good holds and grab quick shakes when you can. Hands down the best route on the wall.

(FA Gary Braaten 1992; 5 bolts)

Kristi Ganz on the classic Frizzle Fry 5.12b. Photo Kevin Sierzega.

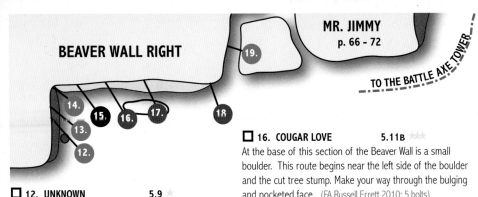

MR. JIMMY
p. 66 – 72

TO THE BATTLE AXE TOWER

BEAVER WALL RIGHT

19.

14. **15.** **16.** **17.** **18.**

13.

12.

☐ **12. UNKNOWN**   **5.9** ✫

Step around the corner from the main wall and head slightly uphill. This route starts just right of the tree. Moderate climbing leads to the tricky bulge encounter. And then another. And another. (FA Unknown; 6 bolts)

☐ **13. UNKNOWN**   **5.9** ✫✫

Directly left of the large chimney is another face climb. This one goes all the way to top! (FA Unknown; 6 bolts)

☐ **14. UNKNOWN**   **5.8** ✫✫✫

Climb the obvious, fun chimney. (FA Unknown; 6 bolts)

☐ **15. DANCE WITH DESTINY**   **5.12B** ✫✫✫

This is the first sport route right of the large chimney. This beautiful and committing route climbs through the prominent vertical seam near the top of the cliff.
(FA Alex Andrews 2001; 5 bolts)

☐ **16. COUGAR LOVE**   **5.11B** ✫✫✫

At the base of this section of the Beaver Wall is a small boulder. This route begins near the left side of the boulder and the cut tree stump. Make your way through the bulging and pocketed face. (FA Russell Errett 2010; 5 bolts)

☐ **17. CATS IN THE CRADLE**   **5.10C** ✫✫✫✫

This route begins on the face right of the base boulder and angles left toward the gully between bolts 4 and 5. Fun and varied with some unexpected surprises!
(FA Jacob Teal 2010; 5 bolts)

☐ **18. LEFT OF THE ARÊTE**   **5.10A** ✫✫✫

Begin on the small ledge to reach the first holds. Climb up the bulging arête. (FA Russell Errett 2010; 5 bolts)

☐ **19. CHIMICHONGA**   **5.8** ✫✫✫

This is the last bolted route on the main cliff and is located in the small hallway formed by the smaller boulder on the North side of the main Mr. Jimmy Boulder. Choose your own adventure and climb the face or stem between the main wall and the adjacent boulder. (FA Jeff Frizzell 2004; 6 bolts)

Nate Battaglia stemming on Chimichonga 5.8. Photo Tracy Battaglia.

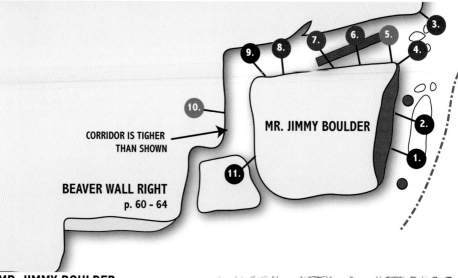

MR. JIMMY BOULDER

The Mr. Jimmy Boulder is to the right of the Beaver Wall and is numbered from left to right as encountered walking into the corridor.

☐ **1. ECHOLOCATION**   **5.12b** ★★

This route follows the left leading band of pockets on the South side of the Mr. Jimmy Boulder.

(FA John Flunker 2008; 6 bolts)

☐ **2. DON'T MESS WITH THE BULL 5.12c** ★★★★

This route begins behind the small cluster of boulders at the base of the Mr. Jimmy Boulder. Ditch your 5.10s and strap on your Air Jordans for this one. Make a serious move for the hueco above the first bolt and battle through some thin stuff on your way to the chains. Keep your cool; you'll want some try-hard left for the top.

(FA Russell Rowlands 1995; 5 bolts)

p. 62. Roger Yee on Everybody Needs Friends 5.12a. Photo Dan Brayack.

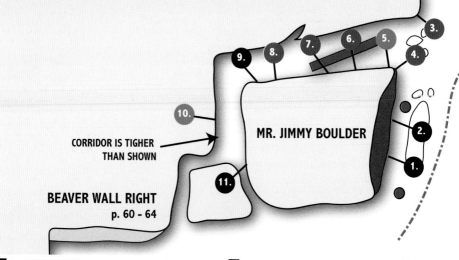

CORRIDOR IS TIGHER
THAN SHOWN

MR. JIMMY BOULDER

BEAVER WALL RIGHT
p. 60 - 64

☐ 3. POINT BLANK   5.11D ★★★

This is the first (partially) bolted route on the main cliff and is located catty-corner from **"BIG WALL GREG'S CHICKEN SHACK."** Perfect for adrenaline junkies on a budget. (FA Mike Balossi 2002; Mixed: 4 bolts + Gear)

☐ 4. PISS ANT   5.11B ★★

This route climbs the left arête of the Mr. Jimmy Boulder. (FA Jeff Frizzell 2003; 6 bolts)

☐ 4A. WHICH SIDE ARE YOU ON   5.10C ★★

Start on **"PISS ANT"** but link right after the fourth bolt into **"BIG WALL GREG'S CHICKEN SHACK."** (FA Dan Caldwell 1998; 6 bolts)

☐ 5. BIG WALL GREG'S CHICKEN SHACK   5.6 ★★★★★

This route ascends the heavily featured slab to the right of the **"PISS ANT"** arête. An enjoyable climb that also offers climbers the opportunity to set up top ropes on some of the more challenging routes on the boulder. (FA Jim Thurmond 1989; 7 bolts)

p. 70. Jon Richard on Spiders from Mars 5.10b. Photo Matthew P. Guempel.

☐ 6. SPIDERS FROM MARS 5.10B ★★★★

Climb the right-facing flake system to reach the second bolt. Mentally prepare yourself and carefully navigate through pockets and smears to gain the brilliant seam feature.

(FA Graham Beecher-Bailey & Chris Schmick 2001; 6 bolts)

☐ 7. VENOM   **5.10A** ★★★★

One of the best slabs, if not the best, at Jackson Falls. Climb the pocketed face until you reach the small roof. Reach through hidden holds to gain the sheer and committing slab above. Expect to fake it with the hands on your way to the chains. (FA Eric Ulner 1997; 7 bolts)

Regina Goldkuhl on Venom 5.10a. Photo Phillip Carrier; Kevin Sierzega Collection.

☐ **8. STINGER**   **5.11D** ★★★★★

This route begins on the short, blunt arête to the right of the small tree. Moderate climbing leads to the ledge that can be mantled to gain a no hands stance. Take a deep breath and tackle the delicate and improbable crux that guards the anchors. Must do!
(FA Eric Ulner 1991; 6 bolts)

☐ **9. VOICE**   **5.12D** ★★★★

This is the breathtaking arête on the far right side of the boulder. Begin on the face between **"STINGER"** and the arête. A short rightward traverse will lead you to the arête. An amazing climb that barely goes; a great introduction to difficult climbing at Jackson Falls.
(FA Eric Ulner 1990; 8 bolts)

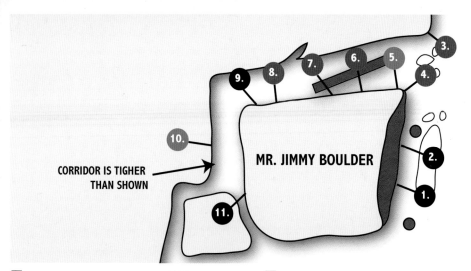

CORRIDOR IS TIGHER
THAN SHOWN

MR. JIMMY BOULDER

☐ **10. LUSCIOUS BABES**   **5.8** ★★★★

This route is on the main cliff and can be found in the hallway formed by the backside of the Mr. Jimmy Boulder and the cliffline. Begin on the dark slab just left of the dihedral. Watch your backside as you scramble up the heavily featured slab. (FA Barbara Knowles, Liz Verkler 1990; 6 bolts)

☐ **11. SPIRIT**   **5.12A** ★

Spirit is the only bolted route on the North side of the Mr. Jimmy Boulder and is directly across from **"CHIMICHONGA."** Climb to the top of the boulder to reach the start. (FA Jim Thurmond 1989; 4 bolts)

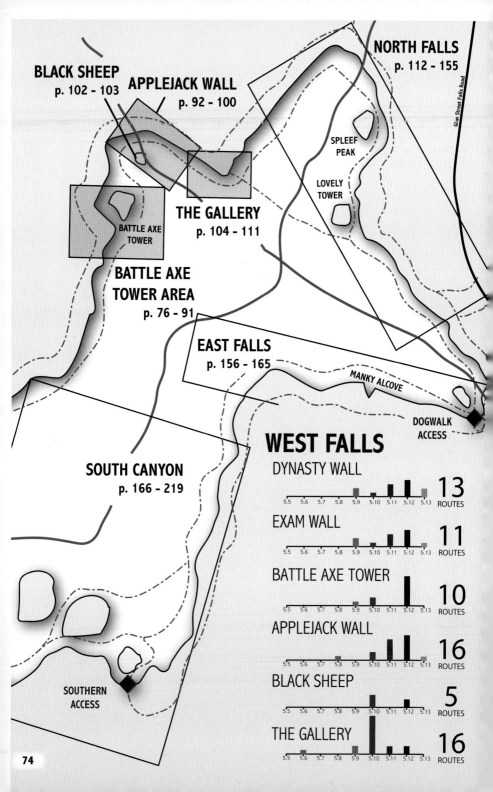

BLACK SHEEP
p. 102 – 103

APPLEJACK WALL
p. 92 – 100

NORTH FALLS
p. 112 – 155

SPLEEF PEAK

LOVELY TOWER

Glen Street Falls Road

THE GALLERY
p. 104 – 111

BATTLE AXE TOWER

BATTLE AXE TOWER AREA
p. 76 – 91

EAST FALLS
p. 156 – 165

MANKY ALCOVE

DOGWALK ACCESS

SOUTH CANYON
p. 166 – 219

WEST FALLS

DYNASTY WALL

| 5.5 | 5.6 | 5.7 | 5.8 | 5.9 | 5.10 | 5.11 | 5.12 | 5.13 |

13 ROUTES

EXAM WALL

| 5.5 | 5.6 | 5.7 | 5.8 | 5.9 | 5.10 | 5.11 | 5.12 | 5.13 |

11 ROUTES

BATTLE AXE TOWER

| 5.5 | 5.6 | 5.7 | 5.8 | 5.9 | 5.10 | 5.11 | 5.12 | 5.13 |

10 ROUTES

APPLEJACK WALL

| 5.5 | 5.6 | 5.7 | 5.8 | 5.9 | 5.10 | 5.11 | 5.12 | 5.13 |

16 ROUTES

BLACK SHEEP

| 5.5 | 5.6 | 5.7 | 5.8 | 5.9 | 5.10 | 5.11 | 5.12 | 5.13 |

5 ROUTES

THE GALLERY

| 5.5 | 5.6 | 5.7 | 5.8 | 5.9 | 5.10 | 5.11 | 5.12 | 5.13 |

16 ROUTES

SOUTHERN ACCESS

JOHN PAYNE

In October of 1985, a meeting was organized to discuss the future of Jackson Falls and the direction in which the burgeoning climbing community was headed. Among those in attendance was John Payne. It was clear to individuals like Payne that this newly discovered canyon had incredible potential. "At one point we looked at each other and thought, 'This place is going to be huge.'"

He was right.

Jackson Falls matured at a point when a monumental shift in climbing was occurring. The introduction and acceptance of bolted protection allowed individuals to focus on the athleticism climbing had to offer. Uninhibited by the conventional challenges associated with traditional protection, individuals were exploring new moves and techniques. "I'll never forget...this guy was climbing Velvet Green 5.12a...and the guy did a back-step. I remember Alan Carrier saying, 'There's that move!' That wasn't part of our repertoire at the time." When climbing became athletic, things changed. "Sport [climbing] became exciting. The shoe technology was exciting. The movement was exciting. The training. The artificial holds. Building your own woody. Lycra was exciting."

However, the technology and practice of climbing were not the only things that were changing. It became clear, albeit gradually, that areas like Jackson Falls were vulnerable and at risk of being restricted. In 1991, the Forest Service began negotiations with the State of Illinois to transfer ownership of Cedar Bluff (a satellite climbing area) to the state. This development brought with it the potential to lose climbing access to one of Southern Illinois' cornerstone crags. The threat of closure made it apparent that without representation and without leadership, the future of climbing in Jackson Falls might also be jeopardized.

In response, Payne and Eric Ulner founded the Southern Illinois Climber's Alliance- a collective of active members of the climbing community. "I knew that you had to make politicians aware of climbing and you had to let the powers that be, whether that be the Forest Service or Illinois Department of Natural Service, know that it was a legitimate activity and not some abhorrent, daredevil behavior. We weren't hang gliders or adrenaline junkies. They missed the point of climbing. We had to educate them."

As a result of Payne's stewardship, climbing as an activity was grandfathered in at Cedar Bluffs. Along with the help of a fledgling Access Fund, Payne continued to work with the Forest Service on projects in other areas including Jackson Falls. The resulting efforts brought with it improvements to the parking lot we know today as well as the road which led to it. "I realized then that there is power in organizing; there is power in a communal voice."

The practice of climbing was changing. The way it was represented needed to change. The way people were enjoying it needed to change. John Payne made that possible. Outside of making climbing possible by providing opportunities in the form of opening new routes, John Payne also legitimized the sport in the eyes of local politicians. John Payne has left and continues to build a legacy as a mentor and leader in the Southern Illinois climbing community.

Photos Matthew P. Guempel.

NOTABLE
FIRST ASCENTS

p. 79. Jon Richard on Emperor of the North 5.13a. Photo Matthew P. Guempel.

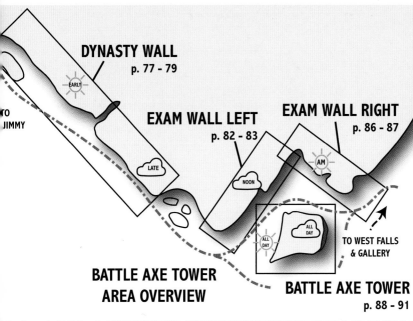

DYNASTY WALL
p. 77 - 79

EARLY

TO JIMMY

EXAM WALL LEFT
p. 82 - 83

LATE

NOON

EXAM WALL RIGHT
p. 86 - 87

AM

ALL DAY

ALL DAY

TO WEST FALLS & GALLERY

BATTLE AXE TOWER AREA OVERVIEW

BATTLE AXE TOWER
p. 88 - 91

DYNASTY WALL

The Dynasty Wall is an amazing section of the cliffline that houses the biggest, baddest routes in the canyon.

The nearby Munchkin Boulder, which offers more moderate climbing, can be found uphill from the main cliffline.

APPROACH

Use the Dog Walk to descend into the canyon. (A detailed description of this descent can be found on p. 31.)

Hike west along the main trail that follows the cliffline. The Dynasty Wall is located around the corner from the Battle Axe Tower area.

The first bolted route you will encounter is route number 13, **"EMPRESS OF THE SOUTH" 5.11A.**

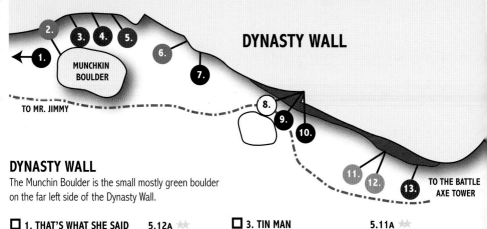

DYNASTY WALL

The Munchin Boulder is the small mostly green boulder on the far left side of the Dynasty Wall.

☐ 1. THAT'S WHAT SHE SAID   5.12A ⭐⭐

Continue along the main trail and hike about 150 yards beyond the Munchkin Boulder. This partially bolted project is located on the main cliffline.
(FA Phillip Carrier 2010; 3 bolts)

☐ 2. THE MUNCHKIN   5.9 ⭐⭐

This route is the only bolted line on the Munchkin Boulder itself. This route can be found by hiking uphill past the main wall through the corridor formed by the mossy boulder and the main cliff. Walk to the back of the hallway and hang a left to find this route.
(FA Alan Carrier 1992; 2 bolts)

☐ 3. TIN MAN   5.11A ⭐⭐

Back on the main cliff, this is the shortest of the three face climbs and is located across from **"THE MUNCHKIN."** This route climbs just right of the gully/crack system
(FA Jacob Teal 2007; 2 bolts)

☐ 4. MIGHTY MOUSE   5.11D ⭐⭐

Start right of the tree and climb the middle line of bolts surrounded by large huecos.   (FA Phillip Carrier 2007; 3 bolts)

☐ 5. MOUSE IN YOUR PANTS   5.10B ⭐⭐

Don't be fooled! The good times on this ride stop abruptly near the top. You've been warned.   (FA Phillip Carrier 2007; 3 bolts)

☐ **6. FLAPPIN' JACK** 5.9 ⋆⋆
This high angle slab stops just below the large roof above.
(FA Karen Clark 2004; 5 bolts)

☐ **7. HYDRAULIC HYENA** 5.12c ⋆⋆
This one is tough even in favorable conditions. Expect to make
some serious moves on bleak holds.
(FA Kipp Trummel 2004; 5 bolts)

The next three routes shared their start.

☐ **8. OPEN PROJECT**
This open project starts on **"FLAIRE"** and **"DSB"** and breaks left.
This line is partially bolted. (Equipped by Chris Loesch; 7 bolts)

☐ **9. FLAIRE** 5.12d ⋆⋆⋆⋆
Follow the obvious flaring seam above the overhanging dihedral.
An amazing feature that begs to be climbed. Good luck, though.
It's rough up there! (FA Jim Thurmond 1997; 5 bolts)

☐ **10. DSB** 5.12d ⋆⋆⋆⋆
The definitive king line: premium stone, sculpted holds and committing moves. Begin on **"FLAIRE"** and traverse right to gain the
remarkable face. (FA Greg Thomas 1997; 8 bolts)

"DYNASTY" and **"EMPEROR OF THE NORTH"** share their start.

☐ **11. DYNASTY** 5.13d ⋆⋆⋆⋆
Likely the hardest route in the canyon. Pull past multiple cruxes
on poor holds with no opportunities to rest. Savage.
(FA Brad Weaver 2006; 9 bolts)

☐ **12. EMPEROR OF THE NORTH** 5.13a ⋆⋆⋆⋆
Bring the big iron for this one. Power through the low crux and
hike through some of the best pocket pulling in the canyon. A
series of low percentage moves on thin holds guard the final run
to the chains. The best of the grade at Jackson Falls.
(FA Rich Bechler 1990; 6 bolts)

☐ **13. EMPRESS OF THE SOUTH** 5.11a ⋆⋆
"EMPEROR OF THE NORTH'S" companion, this route ascends the
broad and featured arête. This one can be difficult to find as it is
often blanketed by moss and other growth.
(FA Chris Schmick 2000; 6 bolts)

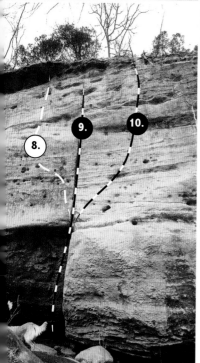

p. 88. Branden Michelkamp on Viking Blood 5.12c. Photo Dan Brayack.

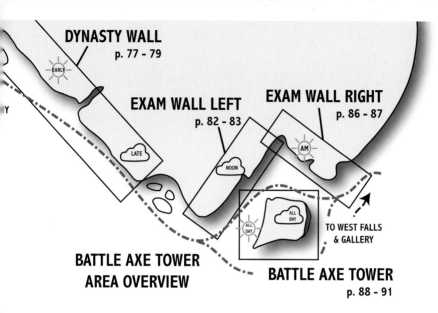

DYNASTY WALL
p. 77 – 79

EXAM WALL LEFT
p. 82 – 83

EXAM WALL RIGHT
p. 86 – 87

EARLY

LATE

NOON

AM

ALL DAY

ALL DAY

TO WEST FALLS & GALLERY

BATTLE AXE TOWER AREA OVERVIEW

BATTLE AXE TOWER
p. 88 – 91

BATTLE AXE TOWER

The Battle Axe Tower and the Exam wall feature the highest concentration of difficult four and five-star routes at Jackson Falls. There's no low hanging fruit here; you'll earn it on classics like **"BURSTING OUT" 5.12c, "VIKING BLOOD" 5.12c, "THE RECKONING" 5.12a,** and **"KING SNAKE" 5.12d.**

The first bolt in the canyon was placed on the left-angling crack in the dihedral between **"KING SNAKE" 5.12d** and **"EAST OF EAST ST. LOUIS" 5.13c.** Climbers at the time referred to this line as "the bolted one" for so long that by the time Jim Thurmond freed the line in 1986, the name officially became **"THE BOLTED ONE" 5.11d.**

APPROACH
Use the Dog Walk to descend into the canyon. (A detailed description of this descent can be found on p. 31.)

Hike West along the main trail that follows the cliffline. Battle Axe tower is located just beyond the West Falls and is quite obvious.

The first bolted route you will encounter is route number 22, **"THE RECKONING" 5.12a.**

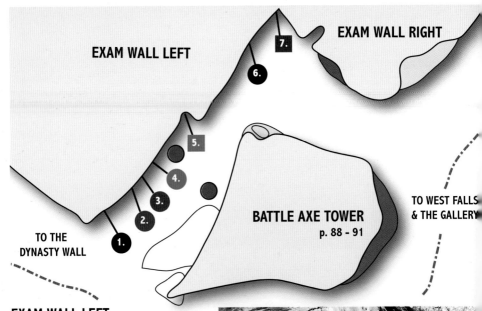

EXAM WALL LEFT

☐ **1. THAI CHI WARRIOR**   **5.12A** ⭐⭐
This is the last bolted route on the cliffline before reaching the Dynasty Wall and can be identified by the faint, left-angling seam. Climb through amazing holds to gain the short-lived but way harder-than-it-looks crux. (FA Chris Loesch 2007; 4 bolts)

☐ **2. TONS OF FUN**   **5.10C** ⭐⭐⭐
This route ascends the large, right-angling flake system. Two, large iron knobs two thirds of the way up the route can help identify this climb. I don't know about tons of fun, but I think it's fair to say "pretty fun." (FA Gene Shertz 1995; 6 bolts)

☐ **3. UNKNOWN**   **5.11A** ⭐⭐⭐
Climb the heavily featured slab until you reach the small bulge near the top. At this point it is likely that you will need to utilize some form of siege tactics to reach the anchors. (FA Unknown; 6 bolts)

☐ **4. THE SOPHOMORE**   **5.9** ⭐⭐⭐
This route is located 15 feet left of the large tree and can be identified by the glue in eye-bolts. Clip the second bolt, then sling good plates along the way until you reach the third and final bolt. (FA Chris Miller 2005; 3 bolts)

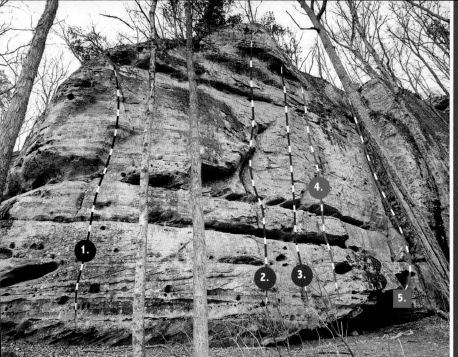

☐ **5. BEAVER BONES**   **5.9** ★★
Climb and plug gear in the obvious dihedral feature
near the large tree. (FA Andy Downen 1989; Gear)

☐ **6. KING SNAKE**   **5.12D** ★★★★
This route is directly to the left of the **"BOLTED ONE"**
dihedral and is the only sport route on this section of
the wall. Punch it hard to connect the dots between
the first and fourth bolt, but tap the brakes when you
reach the technical slab above. This one stays with
you all the way. Don't miss the "snake eyes" hold!
(FA Jeff Frizzel 2005; 7 bolts)

☐ **7. THE BOLTED ONE**   **5.11D** ★★★★
This finger crack is located in the dihedral between
"EAST OF EAST ST. LOUIS" and **"KING SNAKE."** A
perfect splitter on brilliant, golden stone. Bring both
sets of nuts. (FA Jim Thurmond 1986; 1 bolt + Gear)

p. 83. Kevin Sierzega on "King Snake" 5.12d. Photo Kristi Ganz, Kevin Sierzega Collection.

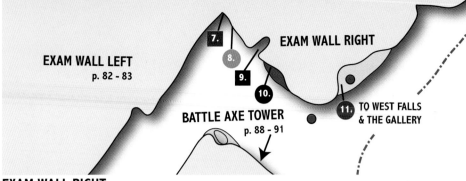

EXAM WALL RIGHT

☐ **8. EAST OF EAST ST. LOUIS   5.13c** ★★★★
A remarkably complicated sequence on impossible
holds leads to the blockbuster crux at the chains.
Savage and stunning, this is one of the best routes
in the canyon. (FA Dave Groth 1990; 6 bolts)

☐ **9. OFF-WIDTH EXAM   5.12a** ★★★
This is the massive off-width chimney that looks
impossible. Looks like a real workout; good luck up
there! (FA Jim Thurmond 1987; Gear)

☐ **10. BURSTING OUT   5.12c** ★★★★
See right.

☐ **11. SPLINTERFACTION   5.11a** ★★★
This route begins on the small platform located directly to the right of the small tree. Follow the series
of right-angling huecos to reach the anchors.
(FA Russell Rowlands 1996; 4 bolts)

☐ 10. **BURSTING OUT**   **5.12c**

This climb is the only sport route located to the right of the large flaring off-width. Thin, technical face climbing leads to an exciting encounter with a brilliant and blunt side pull feature. Grab a quick shake and tear through the small roof that stands between you and the chains. Expect to catch some air if you blow it at the top. (FA Eric Ulner 1990; 6 bolts)

Seibert Tregoning on Bursting Out 5.12c. Photo Matthew P. Guempel.

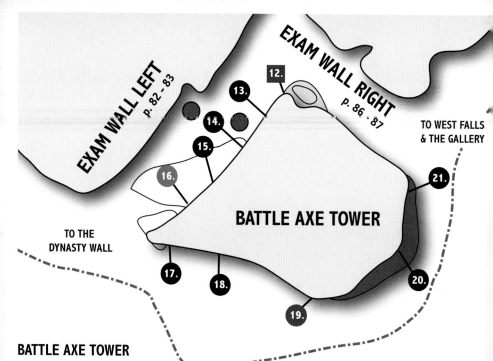

BATTLE AXE TOWER

☐ **12. DOS HOMBRES**   **5.10A** ☆
This route is defined by the miniature detached block
adjacent to the sweeping slab on the Battle Axe Tower.
The first quarter of this route can be protected with
traditional gear (single #2 BD.) The route then follows
the right-angling arête and slab, finishing on the anchor
of **"VIKING BLOOD."** (FA John Payne 1990; 3 bolts + Gear)

☐ **13. VIKING BLOOD**   **5.12c** ☆☆☆☆
Located on the Southwest side of the Battle Axe Tower,
this route is the first bolted sport route on the slab.
Reach through faint pockets to gain more vertical terrain. Edge your way through the delicate and powerful
crimp section to reach the anchor.
(FA Eric Ulner 1988; 5 bolts)

☐ **14. EMINENT DOMAIN**   **5.12D** ☆☆☆☆
Battle through long pulls on thin holds to reach the
heartbreaking redpoint crux that defends the anchors.
(FA 2013; 5 bolts)

☐ **15. THE FLAIL**   **5.12D** ☆☆☆
This route is last proper slab route on this block that
finishes under the far right side of the small roof.
Tough for the shorties! (FA Eric Ulner 1994; 6 bolts)

☐ **16. THE DAGGER**   **5.8** ★★
This route begins with a foot traverse along the base of the slab. Once you have clipped the first bolt, climb the face making occasional use of the arête. (FA Eric Ulner 1988; 6 bolts)

☐ **17. VOID WARRIOR**   **5.12A** ★★
A strange and tenuous start from the detached block will bring you to a good stance. From here, make your way up the technical face.
(FA Gary Braaten 1995; 5 bolts)

☐ **18. IF I COULD FLY**   **5.12B** ★★★
This route is located in the center of the East side of the Battle Axe Tower. Attempt to climb using what appears to be an insufficient number of holds. Fly, levitate, or teleport from the three finger pocket at the second bolt to the large hueco above. (FA Jacek Czyz 2007; 5 bolts)

☐ **19. SOLACE**   **5.10D** ★★
This short face climb can be identified by several huecos surrounding the first bolt.
(FA Maciek Czyz; 3 bolts)

BATTLE AXE TOWER

TO WEST FALLS
& THE GALLERY

Patrick Heddins on The Reckoning 5.12a. Photo Kevin Sierzega.

91

WEST FALLS – BATTLE AXE TOWER

☐ **20. WRECKING BALL 5.12c** ★★★

Punch through sloping huecos down low and head for the blunt, overhanging arête. A hard cross-through on pale holds and pockets leads to more featured stone above.

(FA Dave Groth 1991; 6 bolts)

☐ **21. THE RECKONING**   **5.12A** ★★★★★

Located directly to the left of the detached block on the Northwest corner of the Battle Axe Tower, this route can be identified by the faint, right-facing crescent between the first and third bolts. Be on the lookout for the wine glass and smiley-face holds as you make your way left.

(FA Russell Rowlands 1996; 7 bolts)

p. 100. Jordan Wood on Applejack Crack 5.11b. Photo Jesse Koerner.

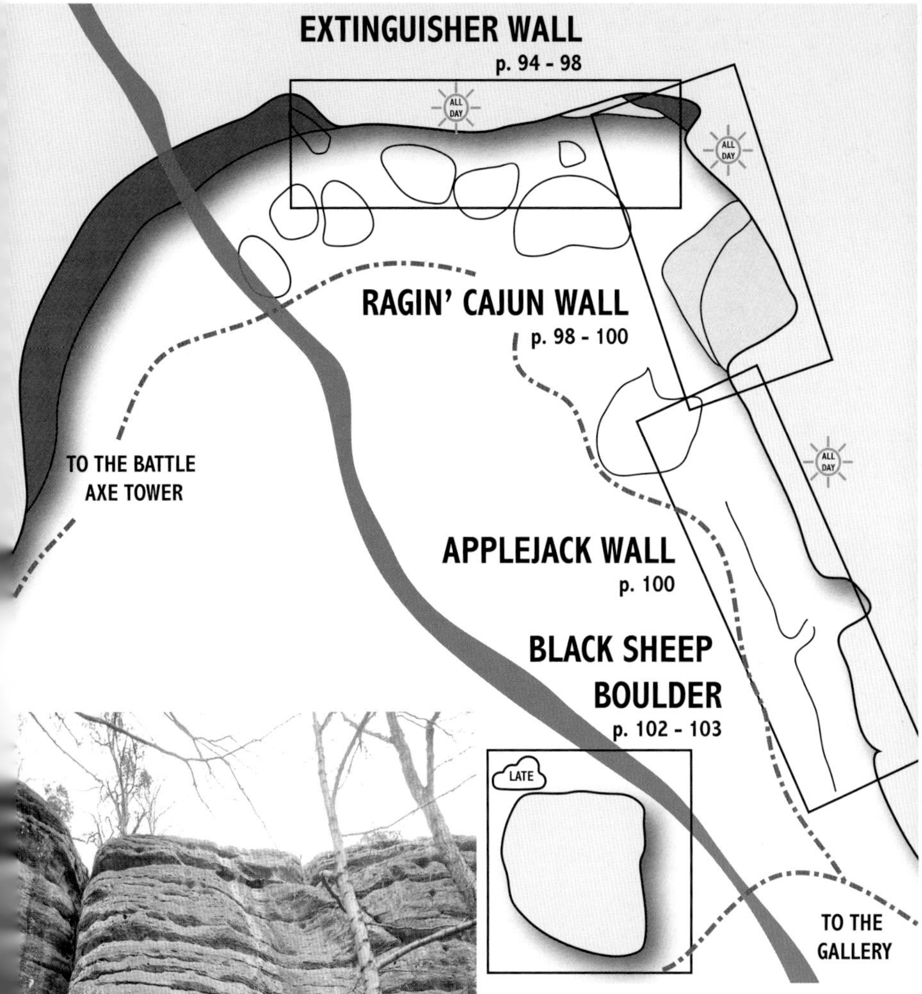

EXTINGUISHER WALL
p. 94 - 98

RAGIN' CAJUN WALL
p. 98 - 100

**TO THE BATTLE
AXE TOWER**

APPLEJACK WALL
p. 100

BLACK SHEEP
BOULDER
p. 102 - 103

LATE

**TO THE
GALLERY**

APPLEJACK AREA

The Applejack Wall can be difficult to spot from the main trail, and as a result, does not receive as much traffic as its neighbor, the Gallery. This area offers great climbing opportunities to those with a firm handle on the 5.12 grade, but routes like **"RIDIN' COWGIRLS" 5.10B** make this an area worth visiting for any climber.

APPROACH

Use the Dog Walk to descend into the canyon. (A detailed description of this descent can be found on p. 31.)

Hike West along the main trail that follows the cliffline. The Applejack Wall is located uphill from the Gallery and adjacent to the West Waterfall.

The first bolted route you will encounter is route number 16, **"STRAY DOG" 5.11B.**

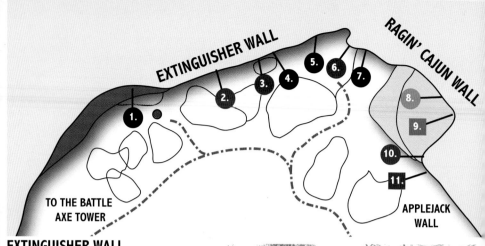

EXTINGUISHER WALL

To reach **"EXTINGUISHER,"** walk along the main trail past the Ragin Cajun Wall. A small trail on your right-hand side will lead you to the Extinguisher Wall.

☐ **1. EXTINGUISHER**   5.12A ★★★★
See right.

A two-bolt extension moves left-ward to another set of anchors (project.)   (FA Chris Schmick 2001; 7 bolts)

☐ **2. RIDIN' COWGIRLS**   5.10B ★★★★
This route climbs through the large, darkly colored water groove on the left side of the wall. Unique holds and thought-provoking movement provide an enjoyable challenge.   (FA Jacob Teal 2007; 6 bolts)

☐ **3. ORION**   5.11D ★★★
This route starts off the small boulder. Tricky climbing off the ground leads to significantly easier terrain.
(FA Phillip Carrier 2007; 3 bolts)

☐ **4. ICE HARVEST**   5.12B ★★★
This route climbs the short face right of the small boulder. Much more challenging that its neighbor, this route climbs through thin holds on perfect stone.
(FA Phillip Carrier 2007; 3 bolts)

☐ **5. AIN'T NO SUNSHINE**   5.12D ★★★
Hike uphill from the previous routes to find this sparsely-featured route. An incredible line with powerful, low-percentage moves on thin holds, monos, and one of the worst slopers in the canyon. "Really hard" would be putting it mildly.   (FA Phillip Carrier 2007; 4 bolts)

☐ **1. EXTINGUISHER**   **5.12A** ★★★★

The perfect route for pocket pullers. Begin on the large, detached ledge beneath the low roof to gain the first holds. (FA Chris Schmick 2001; 5 bolts)

Dan Brayack on Extinquisher 5.12a. Photo Matt Lundberg, Dan Brayack.

p. 94. Phillip Carrier on Ain't No Sunshine 5.12d. Photo Matthew P. Guempel.

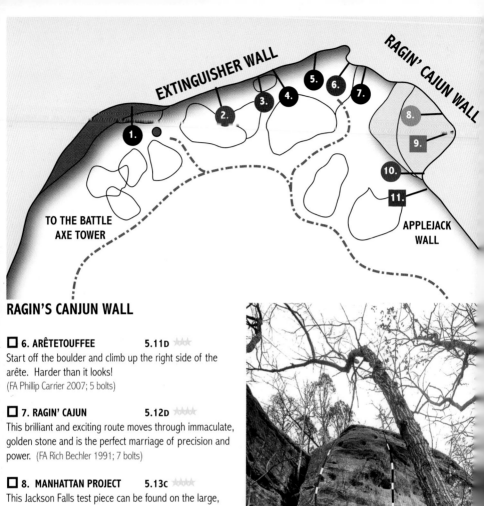

RAGIN'S CANJUN WALL

☐ **6. ARÊTETOUFFEE**   5.11D ★★★
Start off the boulder and climb up the right side of the arête. Harder than it looks!
(FA Phillip Carrier 2007; 5 bolts)

☐ **7. RAGIN' CAJUN**   5.12D ★★★★
This brilliant and exciting route moves through immaculate, golden stone and is the perfect marriage of precision and power. (FA Rich Bechler 1991; 7 bolts)

☐ **8. MANHATTAN PROJECT**   5.13C ★★★★
This Jackson Falls test piece can be found on the large, flat ledge uphill from the Gallery. A difficult boulder problem down low gives way to sustained, punchy climbing. Save some for the top; it's rugged up there.
(FA Brad Weaver 2008; 4 bolts)

☐ **9. BUCKETS OF JAM**   5.8 ★★
Climb the large crack inside the dihedral.
(FA Jim Thurmond 1986; Gear)

☐ **10. BILL & TEE'S EXCELLENT**
          ADVENTURE   5.10B ★★★
This sport climbs ascends the arête to the right of the **"BUCKETS OF JAM"** dihedral. Stick clip the first bolt to avoid the possible and decent spill.
(FA Matt Bliss & Brian Capps 1995; 5 bolts)

Photo Kevin Sierzega.

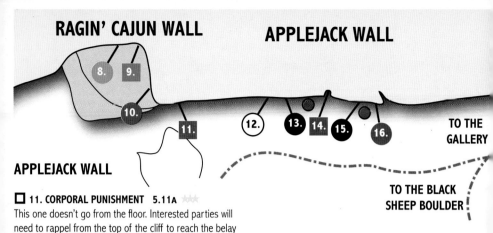

RAGIN' CAJUN WALL

8. **9.**

10.

11.

APPLEJACK WALL

12. **13.** **14.** **15.** **16.**

TO THE GALLERY

APPLEJACK WALL

TO THE BLACK
SHEEP BOULDER

☐ **11. CORPORAL PUNISHMENT 5.11A** ★★★
This one doesn't go from the floor. Interested parties will
need to rappel from the top of the cliff to reach the belay
anchor roughly 30' off the ground.
(FA Eric Ulner & John Payne 1992; Mixed: 2 bolts + gear)

☐ **12. OPEN PROJECT**
This beautiful and sheer face has yet to see an ascent.
Those with a penchant for long pulls between incredibly
thin, almost nonexistent holds have a legitimate shot at the
title. (Equipped by Chris Schmick; 8 bolts)

☐ **13. THE SHOOTIST**   **5.12A** ★★★
This is the first bolted route left of **"APPLEJACK CRACK."**
It does not begin from the floor, and as a result rarely
receives traffic. Rappel from the top of the cliff to reach
the belay anchor roughly 30' off the ground.
(FA Eric Ulner & Greg Thomas 1992; 5 bolts)

☐ **14. APPLEJACK CRACK**   **5.11B** ★★★
This route is the most identifiable feature in this area and
is a good landmark for those trying to get their bearings.
Climb the thin seam that gradually widens into an off-width
crack near the top of the cliff.
(FA Eric Ulner & Miguel Balaguero 1985; Gear)

☐ **15. BIG DOG**   **5.12D** ★★★
Woof. This one is super hard! This face climb is identifiable
by the large depression above the third bolt. An incredible
feature that offers a unique challenge!
(FA Chris Loesch 2008; 7 bolts)

☐ **16. STRAY DOG**   **5.11B** ★★★
This route is left of the large gully that separates the
Gallery from the Applejack Wall. Attempt to negotiate the
obtuse arête while dodging the small tree. Varied and com-
mitting face climbing waits above.
(FA Chris Loesch 2008; 7 bolts)

15.

14.

CHRIS LOESCH

Chris Loesch moved to Carbondale, IL in 2000 from St. Louis, Missouri. Rock climbing as a sport was growing and an entire professional industry around the sport was evolving. The commercialization of rock climbing facilitated the creation of the indoor climbing gym. Indoor facilities began producing stronger, younger climbers who were rapidly redefining what was cutting edge in the sport.

At the same time, the bouldering movement in Southern Illinois was developing steadily due in part to the efforts individuals like Matt Bliss, David Chancellor, his brother Daniel, and Jason Kehl. The discovery of the Holy Boulders in 2001 solidified a movement that eventually secured Illinois as the bouldering mecca of the Midwest.

Naturally, this growing population of new climbers began to explore newly discovered natural resources- often times without proper guidance. The motivation to climb harder overshadowed responsible environmental practices. Irresponsible usage began to change the perspective of individuals like Loesch, "The bouldering scene in Illinois wasn't going well. It was getting bad. As more people started getting out, the more visible user impact became. People left cigarette buts, tape, and other garbage at the boulders which ultimately resulted in closures of areas like Opie's Kitchen."

As a result, in 2002 Loesch, along with a small group of young climbers in the area, broke away from the scene and began to rediscover Jackson Falls. During the bouldering boom, interest in sport climbing had waned, "Not many people had the knowledge to climb on a rope safely. So many people were bouldering at the time that finding someone who knew how to belay was difficult. People weren't sport climbing any more. There were so few people down there [Jackson Falls] that it was rare to see someone climbing routes like Detox Mountain 5.12a or in areas like the Beaver Wall."

Loesch's bouldering experience greatly influenced his approach to sport climbing. Unlike the few sport climbers in the area, Loesch was fascinated with the canyon's hardest routes. "Sport climbing in Jackson Falls is just like bouldering on a rope. Most of the routes are so blank and featureless, that at the time, it was easy to make the transition from bouldering to climbing a rope." Slowly, this new generation of climbers began to resurrect the rich history of the Falls left behind by individuals like Eric Ulner, Rich Bechler, and Chris Schmick.

Inspired by the efforts of key developers like Jeff Frizzell, Loesch began to see potential in other parts of the canyon. Loesch borrowed a hammer drill from a friend and started to revive the spirit of development in Jackson Falls. "Modern sport climbing changed my perspective. Instead of looking for lines that followed a distinct vertical path, it was clear that some featureless sections of the cliff could be climbed if a line that took sharp angles was bolted." Loesch's background in bouldering combined with his outside-the-box-approach led to first ascents of routes like Tai Chi Warrior 5.12a, Duppy Conqueror 5.12d, and Inner Pitbull 5.12d.

Loesch's contribution to Jackson Falls sparked new interest in the area and word of new development brought attention back to the canyon. Like those before him, Chris saw the potential in the notoriously blank and remarkably stunning sandstone that gave you, as he puts it, "exactly enough to get you to the top."

Photos Top: Kevin Todd, Right: Phillip Carrier.

NOTABLE
FIRST ASCENTS

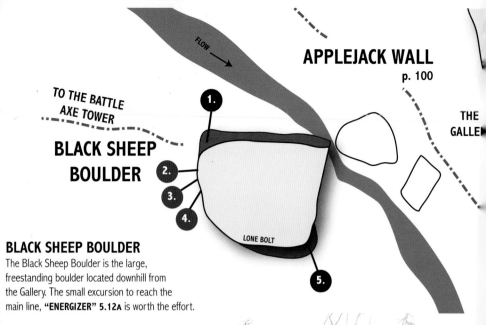

APPLEJACK WALL
p. 100

TO THE BATTLE AXE TOWER

BLACK SHEEP BOULDER

1.

2.

3.

4.

LONE BOLT

5.

THE GALLE

BLACK SHEEP BOULDER

The Black Sheep Boulder is the large, freestanding boulder located downhill from the Gallery. The small excursion to reach the main line, **"ENERGIZER" 5.12A** is worth the effort.

APPROACH

A small trail leading down to the boulder can be found along the main trail as you hike towards the West Waterfall. Cross the stream and turn left to head downhill.

☐ **1. ENERGIZER**   5.12A ★★★★
See right.

The next three routes climb the West face of the Black Sheep Boulder.

☐ **2. THE GOOD**   5.10B
Start on the left side of the angled talus boulder. This is the left of the three. (FA Shawn Watson 2001; 4 bolts)

☐ **3. THE BAD**   5.10C
Start on the flat part of the angled talus boulder. This is the middle of the three. (FA Shawn Watson 2001; 4 bolts)

☐ **4. THE UGLY**   5.10B
Start to the left of the seam/crack. This is the right of the three lines on the mossy face.
(FA Shawn Watson 2001; 3 bolts)

☐ **5. TOUCH MY SHELF**   5.12A ★★
Climb the steep wall near the Southeast corner of the Black Sheep Boulder. This powerful, dynamic route packs a punch! (FA Russell Rowlands 1993; 5 bolts)

☐ **1. ENERGIZER**   **5.12A**

This route ascends the overehanging arête on the Northeast side of the Black Sheep Boulder. Climb through unique holds while trying to ditch the pump along the way.
(FA Chris Schmick 1993; 5 bolts)

Kevin Sarvela motoring up Energizer 5.12a. Photo Dan Brayack.

p. 106. John Payne on Group Therapy 5.10c. Photo Matthew P. Guempel.

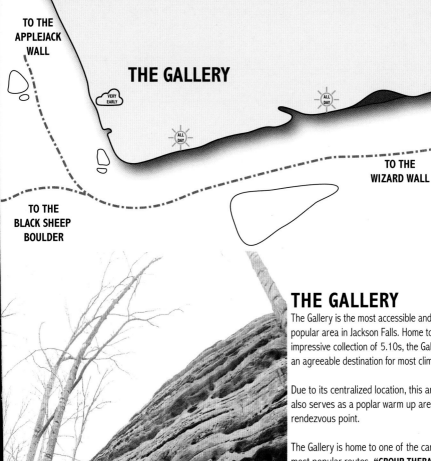

**TO THE
APPLEJACK
WALL**

THE GALLERY

VERY
EARLY

ALL
DAY

ALL
DAY

**TO THE
WIZARD WALL**

**TO THE
BLACK SHEEP
BOULDER**

THE GALLERY
The Gallery is the most accessible and popular area in Jackson Falls. Home to an impressive collection of 5.10s, the Gallery is an agreeable destination for most climbers.

Due to its centralized location, this area also serves as a poplar warm up area and rendezvous point.

The Gallery is home to one of the canyon's most popular routes, **"GROUP THERAPY" 5.10C.**

APPROACH
Use the Dog Walk to descend into the canyon. (A detailed description of this descent can be found on p. 31.)

Hike West along the main trail that follows the cliffline. The Gallery is located past the North Waterfall that feeds into the large plunge pool and creek below. Continue hiking along the trail until you reach the large, dirt clearing.

The first bolted route you will encounter is route number 16, **"NEEDS A NAME" 5.12B.**

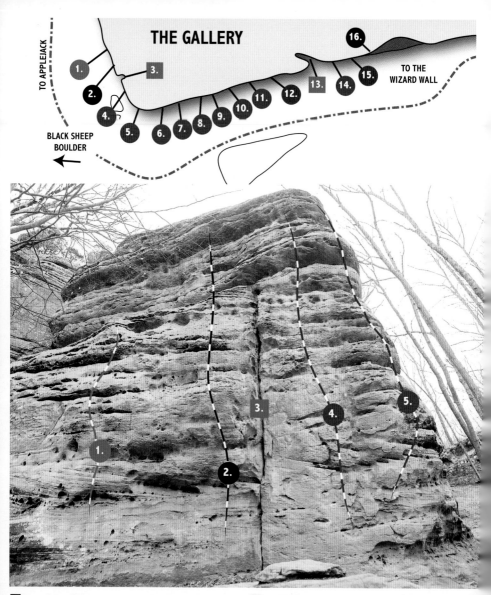

THE GALLERY

TO APPLEJACK

1.
2.
3.
4.
5.
6.
7.
8.
9.
10.
11.
12.
13.
14.
15.
16.

TO THE
WIZARD WALL

BLACK SHEEP
BOULDER

☐ **1. LONE STAR**   **5.9** ★★

The most recent addition to the Gallery, this short route climbs the pocketed face and serves as a nice compliment to the other routes in this area. This route finishes on Metolius Rap Hangers. (FA Jeff Frizzell 2013; 3 bolts)

☐ **2. SHOCK THERAPY**   **5.12A** ★

This route is the bolted route adjacent to **"SQUIRREL HOUSE CRACK"** and can be identified by the large eye-bolts which protect it. Low hanging fruit.
(FA Jim Thurmond 1994; 5 bolts)

☐ **3. SQUIRREL HOUSE CRACK**   **5.9** ★★★

This is the prominent overhanging crack in between the sport routes **"SHOCK THERAPY"** and **"GROUP THERAPY."**
(FA John Payne & Eric Ulner 1986; Gear)

☐ **4. GROUP THERAPY**   **5.10C** ★★★★★

A Jackson Falls standard. This route tackles the golden and gently overhanging stone between the **"SHOCK THERAPY"** crack and the **"PSYCHOTHERAPY"** arête. It doesn't get better than this. (FA Alan Carrier 1989; 6 bolts)

5. PSYCHOTHERAPY   **5.10B** ★★★★
Technical and committing, this line tackles the
bulging arête and can be identified by the large
eye-bolt 15 feet off the ground.
(FA Jim Thurmond 1994; 7 bolts)

6. EARTHBOUND MISFIT   **5.10A** ★★★★
This is the first route around the corner. Unique
holds and varied climbing make this a good
introduction to the style at Jackson Falls.
(FA Lawrence Stuemke 1988; 6 bolts)

7. CUT THROAT   **5.10B** ★★★★
Cruiser climbing on sinker pockets will lead you to a
short encounter with steeper stone at the fourth bolt.
It's easy to overlook some of the better holds on this
one, so be patient! (FA Chris Schmick 1999; 6 bolts)

8. SORE THROAT   **5.10C** ★★★★
This one takes a little more try hard. A brief but powerful pocket section protects the headwall. You'll want to
pump the brakes for the delicate finish that leads to the
anchors. (FA Chris Schmick 1999; 6 bolts)

p. 107. Phillip Carrier on Cut Throat 5.10b. Photo Yusuf Daneshyar.

9. DEEP THROAT   5.10B ✪✪✪

This route climbs through the large scooped impression in the middle of the cliff and shares the start with **"KING'S JESTER."** Climb the large detached flake to reach the high first bolt. Negotiate the steep section and finish on easier climbing above. (FA Chris Schmick 1999; 4 bolts)

10. KING'S JESTER   5.10D ✪✪✪

This route beings on **"DEEP THROAT"** but cuts right to follow the seam between the first and second bolts. (FA Eric Ulner 1987; 3 bolts)

11. THE WALRUS   5.10B ✪✪✪✪

Enjoy the ride on good holds because it won't last long. Start just left of the small tree. Storm the blank and committing sandstone beach above the third bolt to gain the jug you can see, but can't quite reach. Finish on more moderate terrain. (FA Chris Schmick 1999; 5 bolts)

12. YUPPIE WITH A GUN   5.11A ✪✪✪

Start 5 feet right of the small tree and just left of the big tree. Look for the lone pocket located beneath the bulge at the third bolt. This route was the first of the grade in the canyon. Think about that as you make the committing hike to the anchors. (FA Michael Simpson 1987; 4 bolts)

☐ **13. CRINGE CHIMNEY**   **5.6**
Those interested in climbing this wide chimney feature will need to set up a top rope.
(FA Bryan McDonald 1988; TR)

☐ **14. THE MINSTREL**   **5.10c**
Just right of the **"CRINGE CHIMNEY"** is this committing face climb. Don't let the run out at the top steer you away; tie in and keep it together, you'll do fine.
(FA Eric Ulner 1989; 4 bolts)

☐ **15. CRYBABY CLUB**   **5.11D**
Holy shit. This thing is really hard. A baffling and tenuous crux off the ground is followed up with even more perplexing and challenging climbing above.
(FA Jeff Frizzell 2013)

☐ **16. NEEDS A NAME**   **5.12B**
Climb the line of bolts 30 feet right of the crack prior to the large, shelf-like boulder. This one finishes just right of the hanging pine.
(FA Phillip Carrier and Jared Smith 2010; 5 bolts)

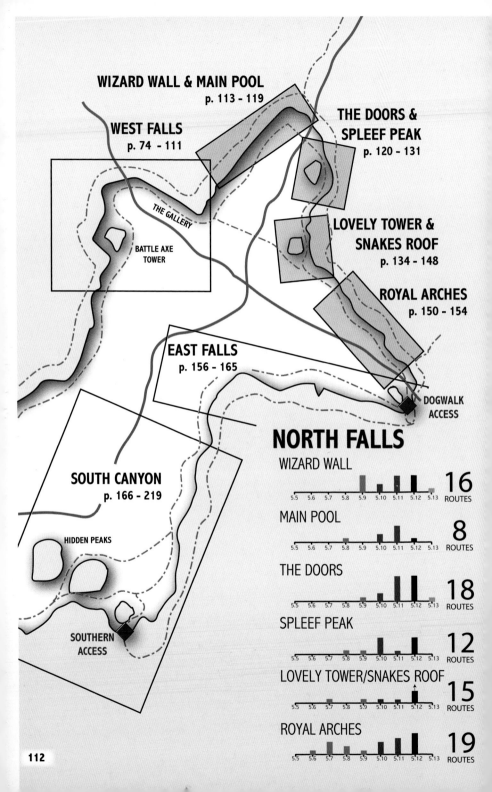

WIZARD WALL & MAIN POOL
p. 113 – 119

WEST FALLS
p. 74 – 111

THE DOORS &
SPLEEF PEAK
p. 120 – 131

THE GALLERY

BATTLE AXE
TOWER

LOVELY TOWER &
SNAKES ROOF
p. 134 – 148

ROYAL ARCHES
p. 150 – 154

EAST FALLS
p. 156 – 165

DOGWALK
ACCESS

NORTH FALLS

SOUTH CANYON
p. 166 – 219

HIDDEN PEAKS

SOUTHERN
ACCESS

WIZARD WALL

5.5 5.6 5.7 5.8 5.9 5.10 5.11 5.12 5.13   **16** ROUTES

MAIN POOL

5.5 5.6 5.7 5.8 5.9 5.10 5.11 5.12 5.13   **8** ROUTES

THE DOORS

5.5 5.6 5.7 5.8 5.9 5.10 5.11 5.12 5.13   **18** ROUTES

SPLEEF PEAK

5.5 5.6 5.7 5.8 5.9 5.10 5.11 5.12 5.13   **12** ROUTES

LOVELY TOWER/SNAKES ROOF

5.5 5.6 5.7 5.8 5.9 5.10 5.11 5.12 5.13   **15** ROUTES

ROYAL ARCHES

5.5 5.6 5.7 5.8 5.9 5.10 5.11 5.12 5.13   **19** ROUTES

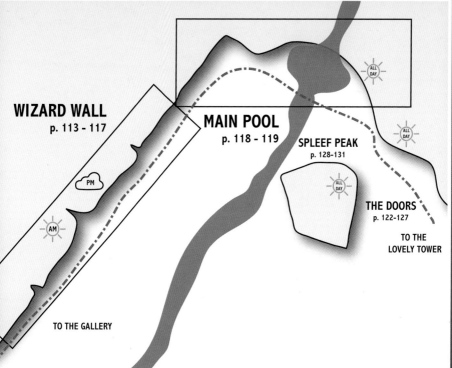

WIZARD WALL
p. 113 - 117

PM

AM

MAIN POOL
p. 118 - 119

SPLEEF PEAK
p. 128-131

ALL DAY

THE DOORS
p. 122-127

ALL DAY

ALL DAY

TO THE
LOVELY TOWER

TO THE GALLERY

WIZARD WALL & MAIN POOL

This area encompasses the routes on the main cliff between the Gallery and the Doors and can be identified by the principal waterfall that is associated with Jackson Falls.

This area stays damp even after brief rain; if you catch it dry don't miss out on classics like **"STAND AND DELIVER" 5.11B** and **"SUSPENDED ANIMATION" 5.9**.

APPROACH

Use the Dog Walk to descend into the canyon. (A detailed description of this descent can be found on p. 31.)

Hike West along the main trail that follows the cliffline until you reach the North Waterfall and the plunge pool below. Just right of the waterfall are routes **"HYDRA" 5.12C** and **"PUFF" 5.11A**. Continue hiking past the plunge pool to locate the other climbs.

The first bolted route you will encounter beyond the North Waterfall is route number 5, **"LOVIN' LIZARDS" 5.8**.

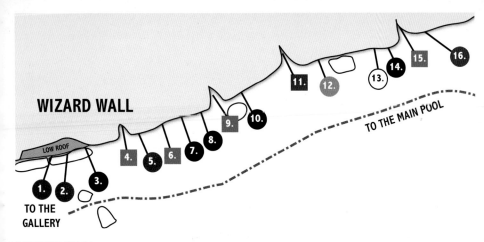

WIZARD WALL

The Wizard Wall features some of the most perplexing routes in the canyon. The wall is named after its principle feature- the flaring chimney which resembles a wizard's hat.

☐ **1. WHAT'S THE DEAL WITH TIM 5.11B** ★★★
This is one of three climbs located in the dark red section of stone above the large horizontal void that divides the base of the cliff. This route can be identified by the glue-in bolts.
(FA Tim Andriakos & Rob Deal 2004; 6 bolts)

☐ **2. STAND AND DELIVER   5.11B** ★★★★★
Some people say that five-star climbing in Southern Illinois starts at 5.12. Put an end to the rumors! This impossibly subtle and rewarding climb is a must do for anyone looking to challenge his or her technical sensibilities.
(FA Dave Downey 2002; 6 bolts)

☐ **3. BROWN RECLUSE   5.12A** ★★★★
This is the last route in the red section of stone above the horizontal break. A tough read, but worth the effort!
(FA Jeff Frizzell 2004; 5 bolts)

☐ **4. DECEPTION   5.9** ★★★★
This route climbs the impressive, winding dihedral crack.
(FA Eric Ulner 1985; Gear)

☐ **5. SPRING ANIMATION   5.11D** ★★
Climb through the small overhang right of **"DECEPTION"** and angle left.   (FA Jacek Czyz 1999; 4 bolts)

☐ **6. SUSPENDED ANIMATION   5.9** ★★★★
This and the following two routes can be identified by a number of water grooves that have created a series of shallow dihedrals. This climb features the large, right-facing dihedral, and has one bolt near the beginning of the climb and another where the dihedral ends.
(FA Lawrence Stuemke & Michael Simpson 1988; Mixed: 2 bolts + Gear)

Photo Kevin Todd.

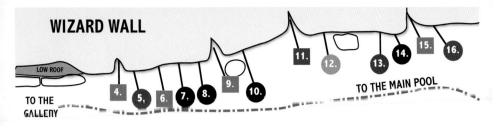

WIZARD WALL

LOW ROOF

TO THE GALLERY

TO THE MAIN POOL

4. 5. 6. 7. 8. 9. 10. 11. 12. 13. 14. 15. 16.

☐ **7. FEMME FATALE**   5.12B ⭐⭐⭐⭐
The quintessential Jackson Falls nail biter. Using a combination of patience and wizardry, inch your way through the faint water groove feature. Contemplating the use of any nylon jugs you may find along the way is completely normal.   (FA Jeff Frizzell 2007; 4 bolts)

☐ **8. T & A**   5.12C ⭐⭐
Start roughly 20 feet left of the **"SETTLED CONTROERSY"** dihedral. Climb over the small boulder and fallen tree to reach the base of this route.
(FA Phillip Carrier 2007 4 bolts)

☐ **9. SETTLED CONTROVERSY**   5.9 ⭐⭐
This route climbs the large, detached flake feature on the right side of the small dihedral. A small triangular boulder beneath the route points towards the climb.
(FA Lawrence Stuemke & Tim Scuras 1988; Mixed: 2 bolts + Gear)

☐ **10. PROJECT**
Where did all the holds go? Climb the face between the two cracks. (Equipped by Phillip Carrier; 4 bolts)

☐ **11. WIZARDS HAT**   5.10A ⭐⭐
Easily the most identifiable feature on the wall. Climb the flaring chimney. (FA Eric Ulner 1985; Gear)

☐ **12. BREAKFAST CLUB**   5.13A ⭐⭐⭐
Located directly left of the large leaning boulder between the **"WIZARD'S HAT"** and **"EAT DIRT"** dihedrals is this challenging face climb. Not for the faint of heart. (FA David Chancellor 2008; 2 bolts)

☐ **13. SKINNY DIPPER**   5.11B ⭐⭐
This is the right-ward trending route located just to the right of the large boulder that rests against the main cliff. (FA Jeff Frizzell 2012, bolts)

☐ 14. STAR POWER　　　　**5.12B** ★★★★

Between the large leaning boulder and the **"EAT DIRT"** dihedral lies this dark red and imposing section of stone. Attempt to find the path of least resistance. (FA Phillip Carrier 2007; 5 bolts)

☐ 15. EAT DIRT　　　　**5.9** ★★★

Climb the wide crack.　(FA Michael Simpson 1987; Gear)

☐ 16. MUD PIE　　　　**5.10C** ★★

This short sport route ascends the blunt arête just right of the **"EAT DIRT"** crack and is protected by three glue-in bolts.　(FA Chris Schmick 2000; 3 bolts)

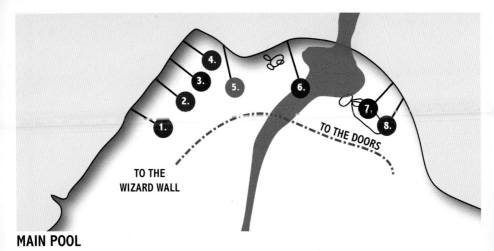

MAIN POOL

☐ 1. ON THIN ICE   5.11A ⭐⭐⭐
Typical Jackson Falls climbing will bring you to a series
of remarkably thin pockets. Resist the urge to pull hard
and carefully make your way through this section to gain
an equally touchy finish. (FA Phillip Carrier 2008; 3 bolts)

☐ 2. BUG MEAT   5.10A ⭐⭐
Just left of the dihedral is this short route. Unlike the
others, this one has been equipped with three glue-in
bolts. (FA Adam Matthews 1988; 3 bolts)

☐ 3. TEMPORARY ESCAPE   5.11A ⭐⭐
This is the first bolted route left of the prominent gully.
(FA Eric Ulner 1987; 3 bolts)

☐ 4. WORKING MAN BLUES   5.10A ⭐⭐
Reach through sparse holds to gain the blunt, left-facing
flake feature. Pull on some pockets and smear your way to
freedom. (FA Jacob Teal 2007; 3 bolts)

☐ 5. LOVIN' LIZARDS   5.8 ✸✸✸
Locals and other Jackson Falls veterans will recall
that this used to be the site of a fixed rope that
allowed visitors to descend into the canyon. Recently,
this route was equipped and can now be climbed in
proper fashion. Despite the grade, this climb may not
be the most accessible for those new to the sport.
(FA Andy Boone & Michael Simpson 1987 bolted by Jacob
Teal and Siebert Tregoning 2010; 3 bolts)

☐ 6. HUECOOL   5.11B ✸
This route is located directly left of the plunge
pool below the North Falls.   This one is sparsely protected and quite short so it would be best to exercise
a modicum of caution.
(FA Tim Toula & Alan Carrier 1988; 2 bolts)

☐ 7. HYDRA   5.12c ✸✸✸
Location, location, location. Not only is this an amazing
climb, it is also scenically located near the waterfall and
just off the main trail. Battle through powerful pulls on
pockets and sloping crimps to reach the anchors. Don't
miss out on the full experience: take this one over the top!
(FA Eric Ulner & Rich Bechler 1990; 3 bolts)

☐ 8. PUFF   5.11A ✸✸
Located on the right hand side of the North Falls, this is
climb serves as a modest compliment to **"HYDRA."**
(FA Michael Simpson 1988; 2 bolts)

p. 124. Jon Richard on Cro-Magnon Warrior 5.12b. Photo Dan Brayack.

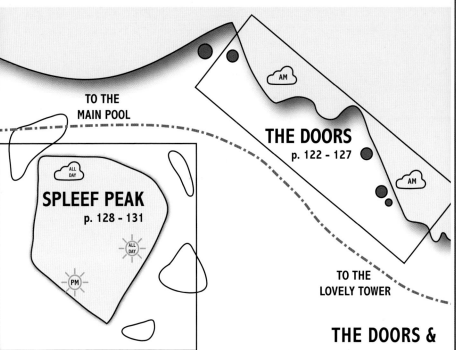

TO THE
MAIN POOL

AM

THE DOORS
p. 122 - 127

AM

SPLEEF PEAK
p. 128 - 131

ALL
DAY

ALL
DAY

PM

TO THE
LOVELY TOWER

THE DOORS & SPLEEF PEAK

The Doors is home of the first bolted sport route in the canyon: **"CRO-MAGNON WARRIOR" 5.12B**. This wall can be identified by its beautiful, rich rust color. Many of the routes on this wall feature thin, incut holds that are not common in the area.

Spleef Peak itself is popular among most visitors; this boulder features routes from 5.8 to 5.12 and is often most people's introduction to climbing at Jackson Falls.

APPROACH
Use the Dog Walk to descend into the canyon. (A detailed description of this descent can be found on p. 31.)

Hike West along the main trail that follows the cliffline. Just beyond Lovely Tower and along the main trail is another freestanding tower. This is Spleef Peak.

The first bolted route you will encounter on the cliffline and just off the trail is route number 17, **"CYBER SEX" 5.12B**.

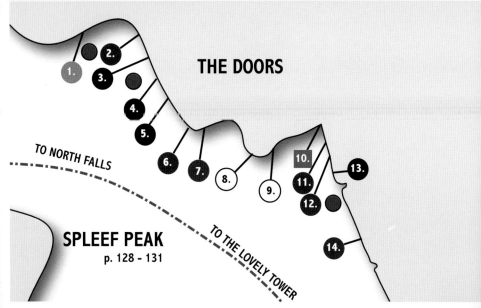

THE DOORS

THE DOORS

☐ **1. AGENT ORANGE**   **5.13A** ⋆⋆⋆
This route is the short and seemingly featureless slab that can be identified by its deep and uniform blood red coloration. Start in front of the large tree, then hope, pray, or wish your way to the anchors.
(FA Matt Bliss 2000; 5 bolts)

☐ **2. LITTLE JOHNNY JEWEL**   **5.11c** ⋆⋆⋆⋆
This understated route climbs the thin face to the right of the dihedral formed by the **"AGENT ORANGE"** slab and the rest of the Doors. This one is rugged from the ground up. Powerful crimp climbing with a punchy finish. Stay stuck!
(FA Jeff Frizzell 2004; 5 bolts)

☐ **3. ANGRY CHILD**   **5.12c** ⋆⋆⋆
This is the bolted route between **"LITTLE JOHNNY JEWEL"** and **"CRO-MAGNON WARRIOR"** and starts in front of the tree. This one comes out swinging and doesn't let up. Expect some heart break at the chains. (FA Greg Thomas 1992; 4 bolts)

Seibert Tregoning on Little Johnny Jewel 5.11c. Photo Dan Brayack.

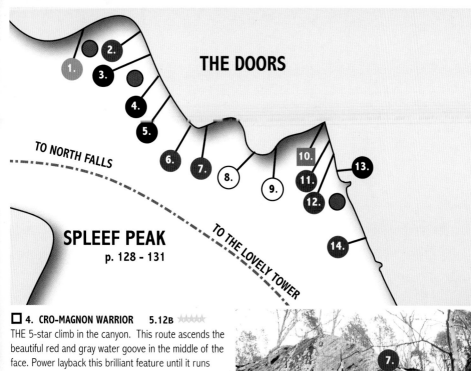

THE DOORS

TO NORTH FALLS

TO THE LOVELY TOWER

SPLEEF PEAK
p. 128 - 131

☐ **4. CRO-MAGNON WARRIOR**   **5.12B** ★★★★★
THE 5-star climb in the canyon. This route ascends the
beautiful red and gray water goove in the middle of the
face. Power layback this brilliant feature until it runs
out. Grab a shake and punch it through some thin face
climbing to reach the anchors.
(FA Eric Ulner, Tim Toula & Jim Thurmond 1986; 5 bolts)

☐ **5. DIGITAL DIRECT**   **5.12C** ★★★★
Just right of **"CRO-MAGNON WARRIOR"** and the large red
streak is this demanding face climb. Battle the low crux
but don't let your guard down on the plated face above;
this one gets thin again.
(FA Jeff Frizzell 2004; 5 bolts)

☐ **6. NO BRAINS**   **5.11D** ★★
This route climbs the pocketed and pebbled face left of
the **"AMOEBA BRAINS"** arête. Expect to make some long
pulls on pockets to reach the more featured face.
(FA Jeff Frizzell 2004; 5 bolts)

☐ **7. AMOEBA BRAINS**   **5.10D** ★★
Don't let the start put you off this route. Pull through
difficult moves to gain passage to the slab above. Enjoy
the run to the anchors. (FA Michael Simpson 1986; 4 bolts)

p. 122. Seibert Tregoning on Little Johnny Jewel 5.11c. Photo Dan Brayack.

125

NORTH FALLS - THE DOORS

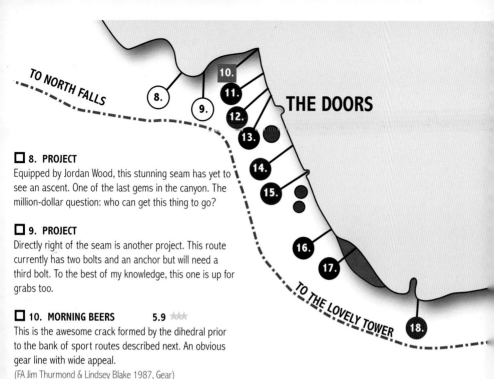

THE DOORS

TO NORTH FALLS

TO THE LOVELY TOWER

☐ **8. PROJECT**

Equipped by Jordan Wood, this stunning seam has yet to see an ascent. One of the last gems in the canyon. The million-dollar question: who can get this thing to go?

☐ **9. PROJECT**

Directly right of the seam is another project. This route currently has two bolts and an anchor but will need a third bolt. To the best of my knowledge, this one is up for grabs too.

☐ **10. MORNING BEERS**   5.9 ★★★

This is the awesome crack formed by the dihedral prior to the bank of sport routes described next. An obvious gear line with wide appeal.

(FA Jim Thurmond & Lindsey Blake 1987, Gear)

☐ **11. THE STAIN**   5.11D ★★

This route, much like the others on this section of the wall, stays wet and is rarely climbable. Despite appearing heavily featured, this one is remarkably thin. Good luck finding holds! Start five feet right of the **"MORNING BEERS"** crack.   (FA Eric Ulner 1987; 5 bolts)

☐ **12. THE TWIST**   5.11C ★★★

An underdog route that grows more and more challenging as you make your way to the anchors. Diverse, varied and totally worth it...if you can catch it dry!

(FA Will Menaker 1987; 4 bolts)

☐ **13. DIAMONDS AND RUST**   5.12B ★★

This route is different in physical character and easy to identify. Look for the dark featureless slab directly right of **"THE TWIST"** and left of the arching crack.

(FA Phillip Carrier 2010; 3 bolts)

☐ **14. FANCY FEET**   5.11B ★★★★

Make your way up the dark face to reach the wide gully at the 4th bolt.   (FA Kathy Ulner 1987; 4 bolts)

☐ **15. BEASTIE**   5.11A ★★★

This massive and beautiful off-width is protected by three bolts. Bring some brass if you want to tangle with this thing.

(FA Kathy Ulner 1989; 3 bolts)

☐ **16. DANCING BEAR**   5.12B ★★

This route begins just as the cliff rounds the edge. Climb the slightly steep and bulging face.

(FA Michael Simpson 1989; 4 bolts)

☐ **17. CYBER SEX**   5.12B ★★★

This route is located off the trail and can be identified by the four eye-bolts that protect the left-angling crack. Climb through positive holds and poor feet to reach a shake at the last bolt. Get organized; the tough stuff starts here.

(FA Chris Miller 1995; 4 bolts)

☐ **18. GOBLIN GIRL**   5.10A ★★

Just right of the big chimney is this route. Climb the bulging arête feature in front of the tree.

(FA Matt Queen 2013; 4 bolts)

SPLEEF PEAK - SOUTH FACE

Spleef Peak is a popular destination for groups of climbers looking for moderates. The south facing slab on this landmark boulder has several routes ranging in difficulty from 5.8 to 5.11!

THE DOORS
p. 122 - 127

☐ **1. MASTER MARLEY**   5.10A ★★★★
On the left side of Spleef Peak's South face is this arête. Fight to keep your body in balance as you make your way up this feature. (FA Jim Thurmond and Mark Newman 1987; 4 bolts)

☐ **2. D-MAN**   5.11A ★★★
This line is the sparsely pocketed and heavily pebbled face. Climb the awesome slab. (FA Bill Rodgers 1987; 4 bolts)

☐ **3. RATTLER**   5.10A ★★★
An incredibly unique feature! Follow the serpentine path formed by the two faint cracks that run parallel to each other. (FA Dave Groth 1990; 3 bolts)

☐ **4. THROUGH THE SMOKE**   5.9 ★★★
See next page.

☐ **5. BLUE SPARK**   5.8 ★★★
Remember those "Choose Your Own Adventure" books? This one is kind of like that. Move between dueling flakes until you reach the third bolt. After negotiating the tricky transition onto the face you'll enjoy the luxury of picking and choosing which holds you'd like to pull on.
(FA Jeff Frizzell, Dave Downey & Dave Kessler 2004; 4 bolts)

☐ **6. THE GARDEN ROUTE**   5.10A ★★★
A great introduction to the double-digit grades! Crimp and smear your way to reach more featured stone above. Remember to drop your heels if your calves start burning! Look for the three glue-in bolts that protect the face just right of the large flake to locate this route.
(FA Jim Thurmond 1987; 3 bolts)

SPLEEF PEAK

SPLEEF PEAK - EAST FACE

☐ **7. SONGS FROM THE WOOD** **5.10A** ✶✶✶

Step around the corner from the previous routes and look for three glue-in bolts. A tough layback section down low will bring you to the much easier and breezier layback section at the second bolt. Expect to catch some air if you blow it on the slab above! (FA Eric Ulner 1988; 3 bolts)

☐ **8. HEAVY HORSES** **5.12C** ✶✶✶

This route climbs the middle of the face and moves left through thin pockets. An ellipsis of huecos at the second bolt will offer a shake before the final march to the chains. This route stops just short of the top.
(FA Michael Simpson 1989; 3 bolts)

☐ **9. STORM WATCH** **5.12C** ✶✶✶✶

This route begins above a small stone block that should encourage you to stick clip the first bolt.
(FA Eric Ulner 1987; 3 bolts)

SPLEEF PEAK - NORTH & WEST FACE

☐ **10. 007 PROJECT**

Closed Project. (Equipped by David Chancellor; 3 bolts)

☐ **11. LOVIN' THE RAIN** **5.12B** ✶✶✶

This can be easily identified by the incredible zig-zagging crack. (FA Jim Thurmond 1987; 3 bolts)

☐ **12. COSMIC BANDITOS** **5.12D** ✶✶✶

Just to right of **"LOVIN' THE RAIN"** is another right-angling crack that eventually thins out. Spoiler alert: if you're wondering if it gets harder, it absolutely does. Brian pioneered the rarely needed and almost never employed head smear during the first ascent. (FA Brian Capps 2010; 5 bolts)

Natalie Rolwes climbing Through the Smoke 5.9. Photo Dan Brayack.

□ **4. THROUGH THE SMOKE** **5.9** ★★★
Climb the right-facing flake just right of the large tree.
Layback, smear and edge your way to freedom.
(FA Jim Thurmond 1987; 4 bolts)

PROTECTING CLIMBING **ACCESS** SINCE 1991

| JOIN US |
WWW.ACCESSFUND.ORG

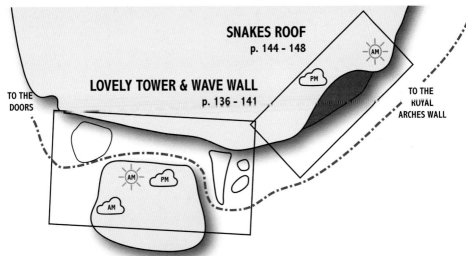

SNAKES ROOF
p. 144 - 148

LOVELY TOWER & WAVE WALL
p. 136 - 141

TO THE
DOORS

TO THE
ROYAL
ARCHES WALL

LOVELY TOWER & SNAKES ROOF

Lovely Tower is the freestanding boulder that forms the corridor with its low-angle counterpart, the Wave Wall. This area is packed with Jackson Falls classics including **"LOVELY ARETE" 5.11A**, **"HIDDEN TREASURE" 5.12A** and the infamous **"FINE NINE" 5.9**.

Around the corner from Lovely Tower is the horizontal roof feature known as Snakes Roof. Originally only one route climbed through the roof, but in recent years it has been outfitted with several additional routes.

APPROACH

Use the Dog Walk to descend into the canyon. (A detailed description of this descent can be found on p. 31.)

Hike West along the main trail that follows the cliffline until you reach the section of the cliff that is capped by a large roof.

The first bolted route you will encounter from the trail is route number 15, **"UMBRELLA GIRLS" 5.12A**.

Kevin Sarvela on the classic Lovely Arête 5.11a. Photo Dan Brayack.

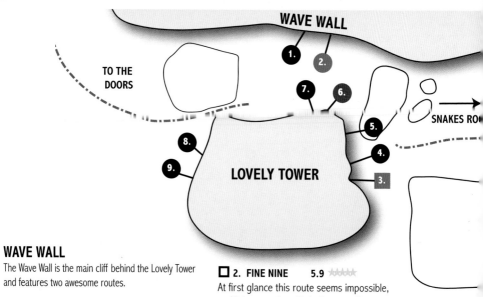

WAVE WALL

TO THE DOORS

SNAKES RO

LOVELY TOWER

WAVE WALL

The Wave Wall is the main cliff behind the Lovely Tower and features two awesome routes.

☐ **1. SPLIT DECISION**   **5.12D** ★★★★

This amazing, improbable slab is undoubtedly the best new addition to Jackson Falls. Look for the three glue in bolts and stick clip the first one. Maybe even the second. And the third. Maybe you should top rope this one first? (FA Phillip Carrier 2008; 3 bolts)

☐ **2. FINE NINE**   **5.9** ★★★★★

At first glance this route seems impossible, and it is more than likely that your first attempt will confirm this initial assessment. However, enough imperfections exist to make an ascent possible. Humbling for most and one that many believe to be a 5.10 (or maybe 5.11) masquerading as a 5.9. (FA Jim Thurmond & Tricia Bowman 1988; 4 bolts)

p. 141. Shawn Cook on Lost Innocence 5.12c. Photo Kevin Todd.

LOVELY TOWER

The Lovely Tower is the incredible free standing pillar that faces toward the main cliff. Don't miss the classics on this block.

☐ 3. LEFTY CRACK   5.7 ★★
Climb the left-angling crack. I wonder what the story behind the name is? (FA Jim Thurmond 1986; Gear)

☐ 4. RAIN DOG   5.12B ★★
Start just right of the left-angling crack and follow pockets up the gently overhanging face.
(FA Rich Bechler 1989; 4 bolts)

☐ 5. VELVET GREEN   5.12A ★★★
Just left of the arête is this often-overlooked face climb. While not as striking as its neighbors, it is still worth the ride. Intriguing holds and baffling sequences await.
(FA Eric Ulner 1989; 4 bolts)

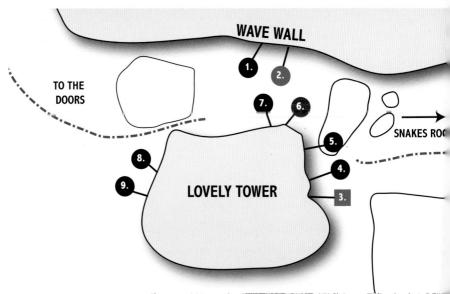

WAVE WALL

1.

2.

TO THE
DOORS

7.

6.

SNAKES ROC

5.

8.

4.

9.

LOVELY TOWER

3.

☐ **6. LOVELY ARÊTE 5.11A** ✦✦✦✦✦
This route ascends the brilliant arête on the
Southeast corner of the Lovely Tower. The
definitive five-star rock climb: an amazing
feature in a beautiful setting, unique holds on
bullet stone, and the perfect compliments of
power and problem solving. Without question
one of the best routes in Jackson Falls.
(FA Jim Thurmond & Alan Carrier 1987; 4 bolts)

☐ **7. HIDDEN TREASURE 5.12A** ✦✦✦✦
Currently this is the only route on the
Northeast face of the Lovely Tower. Climb
through sloping but positive huecos until you
reach the 3rd bolt. Grab a shake, then tear
through the remarkable and thin face. Keep it
together at the top!
(FA Stason Foster 1989; 4 bolts)

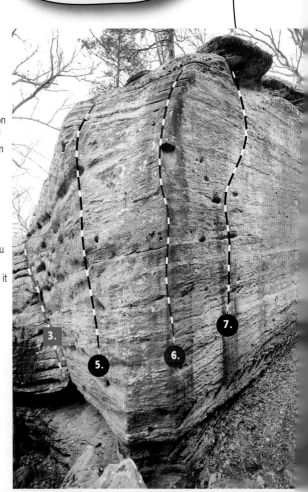

3.

5.

6.

7.

p. 138. Dan Brayack on Hidden Treasure 5.12a. Photo Dan Brayack Collection.

☐ **8. LOST INNOCENCE**   **5.12c** ★★★★
See right.

☐ **9. DISCOVERING SIN**   **5.12c** ★★
A nice addition to the Lovely Tower, this route is a perplexing pocket pulling ride. (FA Jared Smith 2009; 5 bolts)

☐ **8. LOST INNOCENCE**   **5.12c**
Exciting moves between sculpted holds on quality stone. One of the best routes in the canyon.
(FA Greg Thomas 1992; 5 bolts)

Cameron Delligatti on Lost Innocence 5.12c. Photo Kevin Todd.

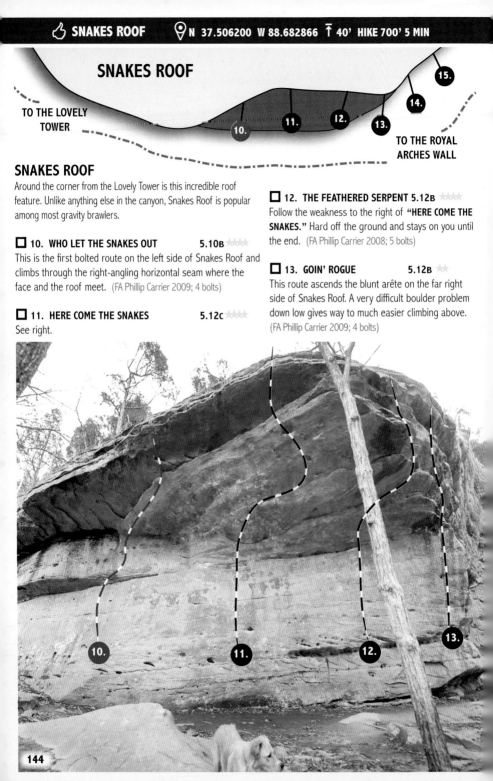

SNAKES ROOF

Around the corner from the Lovely Tower is this incredible roof feature. Unlike anything else in the canyon, Snakes Roof is popular among most gravity brawlers.

☐ **10. WHO LET THE SNAKES OUT**   **5.10B** ★★★★
This is the first bolted route on the left side of Snakes Roof and climbs through the right-angling horizontal seam where the face and the roof meet.   (FA Phillip Carrier 2009; 4 bolts)

☐ **11. HERE COME THE SNAKES**   **5.12C** ★★★★
See right.

☐ **12. THE FEATHERED SERPENT 5.12B** ★★★★
Follow the weakness to the right of **"HERE COME THE SNAKES."** Hard off the ground and stays on you until the end.   (FA Phillip Carrier 2008; 5 bolts)

☐ **13. GOIN' ROGUE**   **5.12B** ★★
This route ascends the blunt arête on the far right side of Snakes Roof. A very difficult boulder problem down low gives way to much easier climbing above.
(FA Phillip Carrier 2009; 4 bolts)

☐ **11. HERE COME THE SNAKES**   **5.12c** ★★★

Until the additions made by Phillip Carrier nearly two decades later, this proved to be the only line through the large roof. Use a combination of gymnastic power and a lot of try hard to tear through the main part of the roof. Have an exit strategy; you can definitely blow it at the top!

(FA Dave Groth 1990; 5 bolts)

Here Come the Snakes 5.12c. Photo Dan Brayack.

☐ **14. UMBRELLA GIRL**   **5.12A** ☆☆☆☆

Just around the corner from the Snakes Roof are two bolted sport routes. **"UMBRELLA GIRL"** is the first route around the corner from **"GOIN' ROGUE."** Start off with a big move to the sloper, then power up the overhaning face through slopers to the final red-point crux going to the chains

(FA Josh Portell 2005; 5 bolts)

☐ **15. INNER PITBULL**   **5.12D** ☆☆☆☆

This route climbs through the stunning rainbow-streaked section of the cliff and features a savage boulder problem near the top. Conditions make a difference on this one so be patient!

(FA Chris Luesch 2005; 4 bolts)

Chris Loesch on Inner Pitbull 5.12d. Photo Jeff Frizzel. Chris Loesch Collection.

p. 153. Natalie Rolwes on Archangel 5.10a.   Photo Dan Brayack.

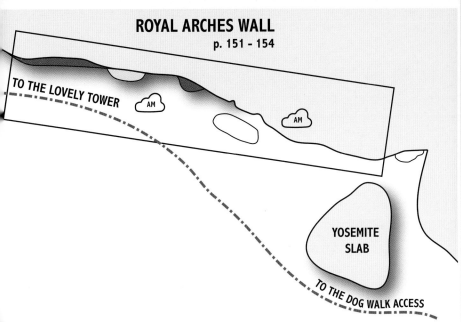

ROYAL ARCHES WALL
p. 151 – 154

TO THE LOVELY TOWER

AM

AM

YOSEMITE SLAB

TO THE DOG WALK ACCESS

ROYAL ARCHES

The Royal Arches Wall is a suitable destination for those new to the sport. Unlike most of the canyon, this area has a number of routes in the 5.7 to 5.9 grades.

More experienced climbers should look to **"ARCHANGEL" 5.10A** and **"THE VOW" 5.11D** for unique and enjoyable challenges.

APPROACH
Use the Dog Walk to descend into the canyon. (A detailed description of this descent can be found on p. 31.)

Hike West along the main trail and cross the stream at the bottom of the hill. Hike past the Yosemite Slab boulder to reach the first bank of bolted routes.

The first bolted route you will encounter from the trail is route number 19, **"EASY GULLY" 5.6**.

David Quinney on the iconic Yosemite Slab. Photo Kevin Sierzega.

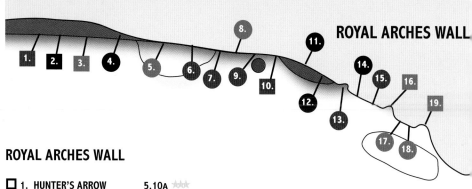

ROYAL ARCHES WALL

☐ **1. HUNTER'S ARROW**   5.10A ★★★
Climb the large chimney.
(FA Jim Thurmond & Hunter Rafferty 1986; Gear)

☐ **2. THE RACONTEUR**   5.12c ★★★
The hardest gear line in the canyon. Make your way through a tough sequence down low to gain the widening crack.   (FA Phillip Carrier 2009; Gear)

☐ **3. HEADING SKILLS OR**
　　 HOSPITAL BILLS   5.8 ★★
This is the third crack system on the wall.
(FA Dan Caldwell 1998; Gear)

☐ **4. NO DOGS ALLOWED**   5.12A ★★
Really sharp and heinous. Battle your way through incut crimps to gain the heavily featured headwall. Though the climbing at this point is considerably easier, it might be best to sling one of the plates to protect the run to the anchors.
(FA Eric Ulner & Jim Thurmond 1989; 5 bolts)

☐ **5. DEETLE DUMPS**   5.8 ★★★★
This route can be identified by the large, left-facing and detached flake system.
(FA Dave Kessler & Jeff Frizzell 2004; 4 bolts)

☐ 6. SUN FLOWER 5.11A

Stick clip the first bolt to avoid taking a spill off the ledge. Inch your way up this baffling slab by side-pulling, contorting and employing the power of positive thinking. This route shares anchors with **"ARCHANGEL."**
(FA Jeff Frizzell 2004; 4 bolts)

☐ 7. ARCHANGEL 5.10A

Unlike the previous two, this one starts from the ground. Palm smear, mantle and use the occasional positive hold to gain the amazing arch feature above. A must do for the 5.10 climber. This route shares anchors with **"SUN FLOWER."** (FA Jeff Frizzell 2004; 6 bolts)

☐ 8. THE MEANEST FLOWER 5.9

Don't let the grade fool you; there's no paddling on good holds to be had on this one. Treat this one like a lady: be gentle, thoughtful, and most importantly pay attention! (FA Jeff Frizzell 2004; 6 bolts)

☐ 9. EBEE 5.10B

This is the last sport route in the dark slab section of the wall prior to the small roof. Start in front of the large tree. (FA Jeff Frizzell & Dave Kessler 2004; 5 bolts)

☐ 10. NO DANCERS 5.11A

This mixed route ascends the crack on the left side of the short roof. Start 5 feet right of the big tree.
(FA Alan Carrier & Mark Oshinski 1988; 2 bolts + Gear)

☐ 11. KRYPTONITE 5.12C

This perplexing route climbs through the three-tiered roof system and requires some serious wizardry. Challenging in unconventional ways.
(FA Jeff Frizzell 2005; 5 bolts)

☐ 12. EXPRESSIONS 5.12A

Find the path of least resistance through the prominent red streak. The small run out at the end keeps things interesting! (FA Eric Ulner 1989; 5 bolts)

☐ 13. THE VOW 5.11D

A spectacular route with unique holds and puzzling moves. Keep your head in the game.
(FA Eric Ulner & Kathy Ulner 1989; 5 bolts)

ROYAL ARCHES WALL

☐ 14. MY HEAD IS BROKE 5.12A ★★★
Start 10 feet right of the **"VOW"** groove. Stick clip the first bolt and climb to the good stance on the ledge above. Try not to blow it as you clip the second bolt. Get organized: this one stays on you all the way to the anchors! (FA Jeff Frizzell 2004; 5 bolts)

☐ 15. KETEK 5.11A ★★★
Multi-pitch bouldering. **Pitch 1**: Tough moves on pockets leads to a challenging mantle. Get it back and prepare for the second pitch. **Pitch 2**: Cruise through positive, but hard to see holds. A tenuous and finicky crux may require you to bivy overnight at the third bolt. (FA Jeff Frizzell 2004; 5 bolts)

☐ 16. PETE'S LEAD 5.7 ★★★
Climb the right-facing detached flake that bears a slight resemblance to a "Bishop" chess piece. (FA Pete Story & Jeff Stallings; Gear)

☐ 17. SMIDGIN 5.7 ★★
Don't let the grade fool you; this one is definitely not for beginners. Carefully make your way up the relatively blank and featureless slab. A 5.7 for the 5.9 climber. (FA Adam Matthews 1987; 6 bolts)

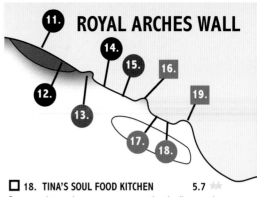

ROYAL ARCHES WALL

☐ 18. TINA'S SOUL FOOD KITCHEN 5.7 ★★
Smear, palm, and press your way up the rippling sandstone slab. (FA Tina Carpenter & Bill Rodgers 1981; 6 bolts)

☐ 19. EASY GULLY 5.6 ★
Top rope only. Begin on the slab and climb right toward the large gully. (FA Eric Ulner 1981; Top Rope)

p. 153. Kevin Sarvela on The Vow 5.11d. Photo Dan Brayack.

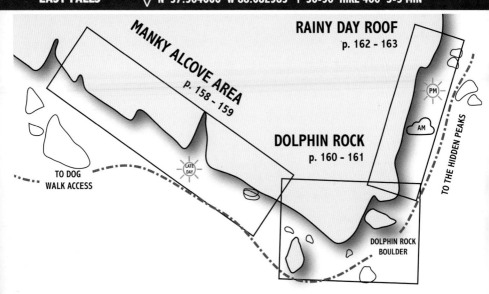

MANKY ALCOVE AREA
p. 158 - 159

RAINY DAY ROOF
p. 162 - 163

DOLPHIN ROCK
p. 160 - 161

TO DOG
WALK ACCESS

TO THE HIDDEN PEAKS

DOLPHIN ROCK
BOULDER

EAST FALLS AREA

"East Falls" describes the three smaller climbing areas between the Dog Walk access and Hidden Peaks. Despite their height and lack of diversity, Manky Alcove, Dolphin Rock, and Rainy Day Roof should not be overlooked.

APPROACH

Use the Dog Walk to descend into the canyon. (A detailed description of this descent can be found on p. 31.)

At the bottom of the Dog Walk is a narrow corridor capped by a boulder. Walk through the cave to rejoin the trail.

The first area you will encounter is the Manky Alcove.

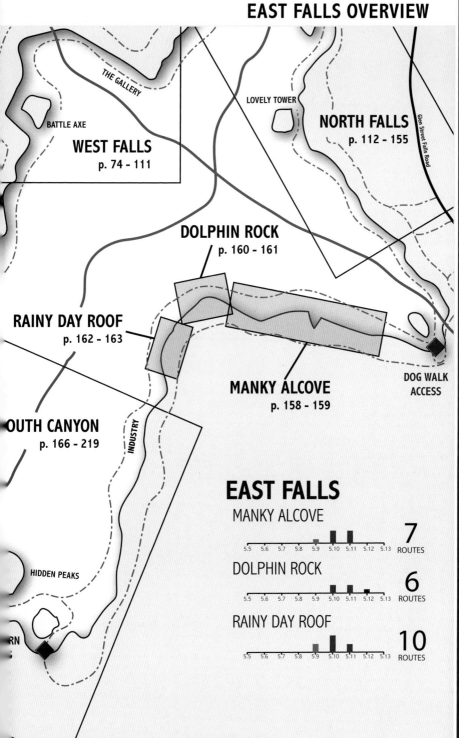

THE GALLERY

BATTLE AXE

LOVELY TOWER

WEST FALLS
p. 74 – 111

NORTH FALLS
p. 112 – 155

Glen Street Falls Road

DOLPHIN ROCK
p. 160 – 161

RAINY DAY ROOF
p. 162 – 163

DOG WALK
ACCESS

MANKY ALCOVE
p. 158 – 159

OUTH CANYON
p. 166 – 219

INDUSTRY

HIDDEN PEAKS

RN

EAST FALLS

MANKY ALCOVE

5.5 | 5.6 | 5.7 | 5.8 | 5.9 | 5.10 | 5.11 | 5.12 | 5.13

7 ROUTES

DOLPHIN ROCK

5.5 | 5.6 | 5.7 | 5.8 | 5.9 | 5.10 | 5.11 | 5.12 | 5.13

6 ROUTES

RAINY DAY ROOF

5.5 | 5.6 | 5.7 | 5.8 | 5.9 | 5.10 | 5.11 | 5.12 | 5.13

10 ROUTES

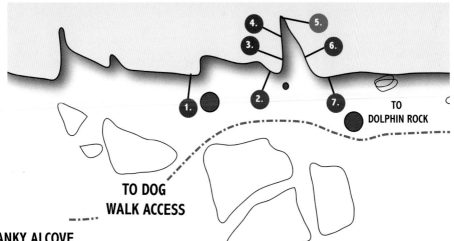

TO
DOLPHIN ROCK

TO DOG
WALK ACCESS

MANKY ALCOVE

Aptly named, this is the dark and damp alcove located just off the main trail. Look for the dagger-like feature in the back of the hallway. This is the area's main attraction, **"ESSENCE OF MANKY" 5.9.**

The first route you will encounter from the trail is route number 1, **"CHUCK-O-RAMA" 5.11D**.

☐ **1. CHUCK-O-RAMA**   **5.11D** ⭐⭐
This route is not actually located in the alcove itself, but on the vertical section of the cliff prior to it. Locate the sharp arête adjacent to the large off-width dihedral. This route climbs the face left of the arête and features a large break near the halfway point.
(FA Ray Whaley & Stuart Johnson 1995; 5 bolts)

☐ **2. SLUG MAN**   **5.10B** ⭐
Climb the slab directly left of the corridor's entrance. This route shares anchors with **"HUNGRY WOLF."**
(FA Ray Whaley 1992; 3 bolts)

☐ **3. HUNGRY WOLF**   **5.11A** ⭐
This route is located on the left side of the corridor and shares anchors with **"SLUG MAN."** Climb through the fain left-angling seam that gradually opens up near the third bolt. Consider stick clipping the second bolt before tying in.
(FA Jeff Frizzell 2004; 4 bolts)

☐ **4. ACCESS DENIED**   **5.11C** ⭐
Also on the left side of the corridor; climb the sheer face right of the prominent red streak.
(FA Ray Whaley 1992; 4 bolts)

Brian Kelley on Essence of Manky 5.9.
Photo Matthew P. Guempel.

☐ **5. ESSENCE OF MANKY**   **5.9** ★★

At the back of the alcove is a dagger-like section of stone wedged between the corridor's two walls. Stem and press your way to the anchors below the overhang above. If there's a "must-do" in the alcove, it's this one.
(FA Jim Thurmond & Eric Ulner 1985; 4 bolts)

☐ **6. CREEP SHOW**   **5.10A** ★

This is the only bolted route on the right side of the hallway.   (FA Ray Whaley 1992; 3 bolts)

☐ **7. BIG BROTHER**   **5.10B** ★

Outside of the hallway on the right hand side is this diminutive slab. Climb the scooped out face clipping glue-in bolts along the way.
(FA Phillip Carrier 2008; 4 bolts)

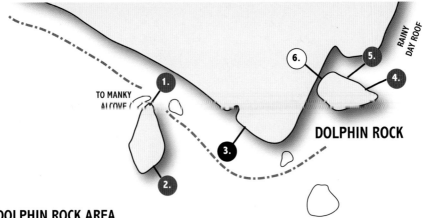

DOLPHIN ROCK AREA

This area includes the two house-sized boulders along the trail, as well as a single sport route on the main cliff.

Those who are new to the area may want to consider exploring other parts of the canyon first before making a pit stop here.

The first route you will encounter from the trail is route number 1, **"NEEDS A NAME" 5.10B.**

☐ **1. NEEDS A NAME   5.10B** ☆☆
Hike South (away from the Dog Walk Access) along the trail and locate the large overhanging boulder on the right side of the trail just beyond Manky Alcove. This route begins with the short arête and makes its way through the overhang.   (FA Phillip Carrier 2012; 4 bolts)

☐ **2. TREE HUGGER   5.11B** ☆☆
On the backside of the same boulder is another sport route. Hike downhill from **"NEEDS A NAME"** and turn right.   (FA Phillip Carrier 2007; 4 bolts)

☐ **3. FRED & WILMA   5.12B** ☆☆
Just beyond the Manky Alcove the main cliffline takes a sharp left turn. Prior to where the cliff turns the corner is a two-tiered, rust colored streak just right of the large gully. Look for the large and lonely pocket to identify this route.   (FA Jim Schneider & Margie Belt 1999; 5 bolts)

☐ **4. JIMMY GILLESPIE   5.11A** ☆☆
This is the first route you will encounter upon entering the hallway. Swim through the sea of sandstone pockets to reach the anchor at the top of the boulder.
(FA Dan Smith 2000; 3 bolts)

□ 5. DOLPHIN FRIENDLY   **5.10A** ⭐⭐

Moderate and enjoyable climbing leads to a break near the top. Stop here to get it back or keep cruising.

(FA Unknown; 3 bolts)

□ 6. UNKNOWN

This route is on the same boulder as the previous lines and can be found by walking to the back of the hallway. Hang a left and turn the corner.

(FA Unknown; 3 bolts)

DOLPHIN ROCK

RAINY DAY ROOF

TO THE
INDUSTRY WALL

RAINY DAY ROOF

Perfect on days after a strong rain, this is the only wall in the canyon guaranteed to stay dry. Despite being short, these routes are remarkably fun and challenging.

The first route you will encounter from the trail is route number 1, **"SWEET LEAF"** 5.9.

☐ **1. SWEET LEAF** **5.9** ⋆⋆
Climb the short, bulging face just left of the large detached flake feature. Look for the tan hangers.
(FA Leif Faber 2013; 3 bolts)

☐ **2. PROJECT**
Currently a closed project. (Equipped by Chris Loesch; 2 bolts)

☐ **3. FLASH** **5.10c** ⋆⋆⋆
This savage crimp line can be identified by the dark ink stain that bleeds from the anchors. Thin climbing leads to even thinner climbing. Take advantage of the occasional sinker hold to keep it together and get organized.
(FA Chris Schmick 1998; 3 bolts)

☐ **4. LIGHTNING** **5.10b** ⋆⋆
More featured than the previous line, this one gets you high and then makes you cry. Sloped holds at the run to the anchor make for a reasonably committing finish.
(FA Chris Schmick 1998; 3 bolts)

☐ **5. THUNDER** **5.11a** ⋆
This one puts the "sand" into "sandbagged!" The anchor may be difficult to see from the ground; it's above the bulge.
(FA Chris Schmick 1998; 3 bolts)

☐ **6. ZAPPED** **5.11a** ⋆⋆⋆
Left of the small dihedral, this route starts by climbing the short-lived steep section. Long pulls between sinker holds make this the most popular line on the wall.
(FA Matt Bliss 1998; 3 bolts)

☐ **7. FAT AND SASSY** **5.9** ⋆⋆
This is the first bolted route just right of the small dihedral beneath the Rainy Day Roof. Climb the left-facing and heavily featured flake. (FA Phillip Carrier and Jared Smith 2009; 3 bolts)

Sarah Laine on Lightning 5.10B.
Photo Matthew P. Guempel.

☐ **8. SILVER LINING** **5.10b** ⋆⋆
A low crux is followed up with more manageable terrain. (FA Jeff Frizzell 2013; 4 bolts)

☐ **9. RAISE THE ROOF** **5.10b** ⋆⋆
This is the only route that goes all the way to the top! Pull through tricky moves on the face and finish on steeper climbing. (FA Phillip Carrier 2013, 6 bolts)

☐ **10. PROJECT**
This project is currently red tagged but has not been fully equipped. (Equipped by Jeff Frizzell)

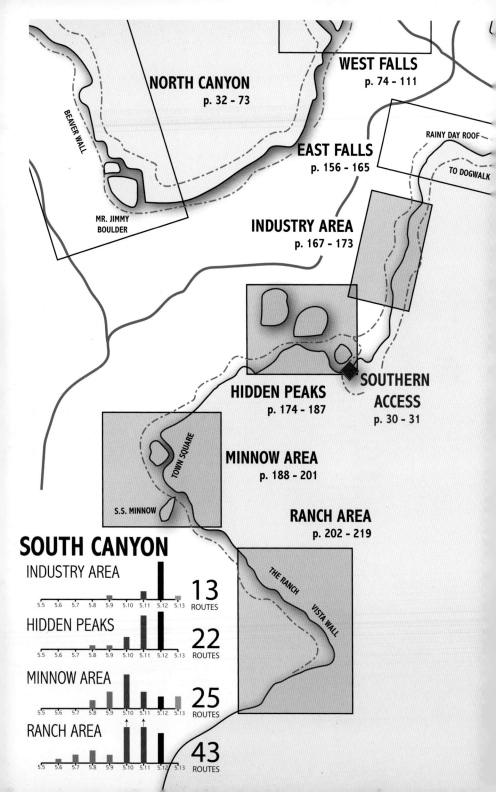

NORTH CANYON
p. 32 – 73

BEAVER WALL

MR. JIMMY BOULDER

WEST FALLS
p. 74 – 111

RAINY DAY ROOF

TO DOGWALK

EAST FALLS
p. 156 – 165

INDUSTRY AREA
p. 167 – 173

HIDDEN PEAKS
p. 174 – 187

SOUTHERN ACCESS
p. 30 – 31

TOWN SQUARE

MINNOW AREA
p. 188 – 201

S.S. MINNOW

RANCH AREA
p. 202 – 219

THE RANCH

VISTA WALL

SOUTH CANYON

INDUSTRY AREA

5.5 5.6 5.7 5.8 5.9 5.10 5.11 5.12 5.13

13 ROUTES

HIDDEN PEAKS

5.5 5.6 5.7 5.8 5.9 5.10 5.11 5.12 5.13

22 ROUTES

MINNOW AREA

5.5 5.6 5.7 5.8 5.9 5.10 5.11 5.12 5.13

25 ROUTES

RANCH AREA

5.5 5.6 5.7 5.8 5.9 5.10 5.11 5.12 5.13

43 ROUTES

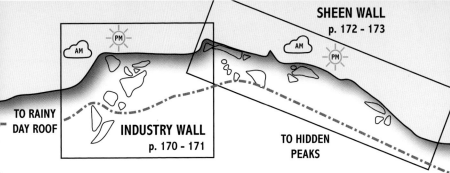

SHEEN WALL
p. 172 – 173

TO RAINY
DAY ROOF

INDUSTRY WALL
p. 170 – 171

TO HIDDEN
PEAKS

AM   PM   AM   PM

INDUSTRY AREA

This area describes the bank of routes located between Rainy Day Roof and Hidden Peaks. While this area does not have as high a concentration as other areas, it is definitely worth the stop.

"INDUSTRY" 5.12A and **"AUTOMATIC DAMNATION" 5.11C** are must-do routes!

APPROACH

Use the Dog Walk to descend into the canyon. (A detailed description of this descent can be found on p. 31.)

Hike past Rainy Day Roof; the cliffline will make a sharp left turn.

The first bolted route you will encounter from the trail is route number 1, **"INDUSTRY" 5.12A.**

Photo Kevin Sierzega.

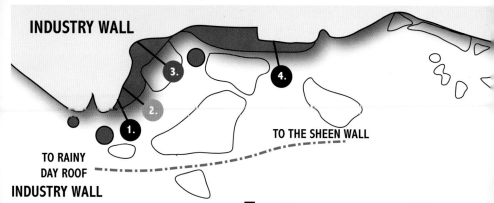

INDUSTRY WALL

INDUSTRY WALL

☐ **1. INDUSTRY**   **5.12A** ✶✶✶
Race up the steep face in an effort to avoid the unexpected pump that will make pulling the lip almost impossible. Don't worry if you blow it at the top; we all have. This route shares anchors with **"PULSE."**
(FA Doug Fritz & Scott Swanson 1995; 3 bolts)

☐ **2. PULSE**   **5.13A** ✶✶
Directly right of **"INDUSTRY"** is its burly counterpart. Punch it hard through positive holds until they run out. Grab the worst holds ever and head over the top. This route shares anchors with **"INDUSTRY."**   (FA Matt Bliss 1999; 4 bolts)

☐ **3. AUTOMATIC DAMNATION**   **5.11c** ✶✶✶✶
Exciting, varied, and unlike any other route in canyon. Power layback the flake system at the halfway point to gain the roof crack. Use brains and brawn (but mostly brawn) to take this one to the chains!
(FA Phillip Carrier 2011; 7 bolts)

☐ **4. OPTICAL CONCLUSION**   **5.12A** ✶✶✶
Past the corridor formed by collection of boulders beneath **"AUTOMATIC DAMNNATION"** is this sport climbing adventure. Look for the large, rounded undercling feature at the second bolt to identify this route.
(FA Eric Heuermann 2004; 7 bolts)

Ian Anderson on Automatic Damnation 5.11c. Photo Matthew P. Guempel.

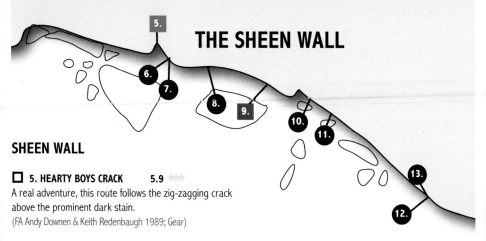

THE SHEEN WALL

SHEEN WALL

☐ **5. HEARTY BOYS CRACK**   **5.9** ✭✭✭
A real adventure, this route follows the zig-zagging crack above the prominent dark stain.
(FA Andy Downen & Keith Redenbaugh 1989; Gear)

☐ **6. AGGRO-SHEEN**   **5.12B** ✭✭✭
Climb the face just right of the **"HEARTY BOYS' CRACK."** Clip the third bolt and break left to the seperate set of anchors.   (FA Chris Schmick 2001; 6 bolts)

☐ **7. AGGRO-SHEEN DIRECT**   **5.12C** ✭✭✭✭
Begin on **"AGGRO-SHEEN"** but continue straight up the face. Take a deep breath and get ready to dive in.
(FA Chris Schmick 2001; 5 bolts)

☐ **8. WATCH DOG**   **5.12A** ✭✭
This route is tucked behind a massive boulder. Begin on the small boulder and delicately work your way up the face and left.   (FA Eric Ulner, John Sommerhof 1995; 6 bolts)

☐ **9. THE DIGGLER**   **5.11D** ✭✭✭
Climb the right-angling crack using small to mid sized gear, climbing past two bolts to the anchor.
(FA Dan Caldwell 2000; Gear + 2 bolts)

Photo Kevin Sierzega

Photo Kevin Sierzega.

☐ **10. UNKNOWN**   **5.12c** ★★
A crux at the bulge is followed by a second on the slab above.
(FA Jared Smith; 5 bolts)

☐ **11. INIQUITY**   **5.12A** ★★★
Look for the three eye-bolts that protect the first half of this route.
(FA Kipp Trummel 2004; 6 bolts)

The next two routes share the first five bolts, then split.

☐ **12. OCD**   **5.12D** ★★★★
While Obsessive Climbing Disorder (or OCD) is untreatable, it can be managed with a combination of physical therapy and self-medication.

Climb the steep face and cut left at the 5th bolt. Get the lead out for the final push. (FA Chris Loesch 2010; 6 bolts)

☐ **13. ADDICTION**   **5.12c** ★★★★
Begin on OCD but head straight up at the 5th bolt. These routes are often wet, making opportunities for a good burn few and far between. If you catch them during a dry spell, you won't be disappointed! (FA Chris Loesch 2010; 7 bolts)

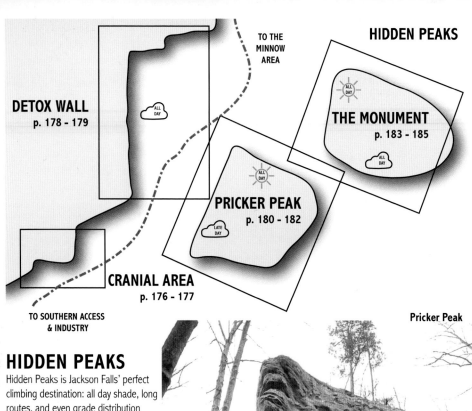

TO THE
MINNOW
AREA

HIDDEN PEAKS

DETOX WALL
p. 178 - 179

ALL
DAY

THE MONUMENT
p. 183 - 185

ALL
DAY

ALL
DAY

ALL
DAY

PRICKER PEAK
p. 180 - 182

LATE
DAY

CRANIAL AREA
p. 176 - 177

TO SOUTHERN ACCESS
& INDUSTRY

Pricker Peak

HIDDEN PEAKS

Hidden Peaks is Jackson Falls' perfect climbing destination: all day shade, long routes, and even grade distribution make this a popular area. You can easily spend an entire day climbing routes on the main wall and the three satellite boulders that make up the area.

Popular routes include **"DETOX MOUNTAIN" 5.12A, "STUBBORN SWEDE" 5.8 AND "CHEERIO BOWL" 5.10A.**

APPROACH

Hike towards the Dog Walk Descent. Rather than descending here, hike South along the top trail to reach the Southern Access. (A detailed description of this descent can be found on p. 31.)

p. 178. Sarah Laine on Detox Mountain 5.12a. Photo Matthew P. Guempel.

CRANIAL WALL

DETOX WALL

ALTERNATE TO
SOUTHERN ACCESS

1.

2.

3.

TO SOUTHERN
ACCESS

TO HIDDEN PEAKS

☐ **1. KAYA**   **5.12c**
This route is located near the base of the ravine that leads
to the top trail. Climb the short and disappointing face.
(FA Mark Polino 1998; 4 bolts)

☐ **2. CRANIAL IMPLOSION**   **5.12a**
Pull on one bad hold to earn your points. Not a plum line,
but worth a shot if you need to fill out that tick list.
(FA Scott Swanson 1995; 4 bolts)

Cameron Delligatti on Cranial Implosion 5.12a. Photo Kevin Todd.

DETOX WALL

☐ 3. COCKTAIL GENERATION   5.12B ★★

This route climbs the tall and vertical face on the left side of the main wall. Moderate climbing leads to a break where it would be in your best interest to grab a shake. Fire through two brief, consecutive cruxes to gain easier ground above. (FA Jeff Frizzel 2008; 5 bolts)

☐ 4. ELDERS OF THE TRIBE   5.12C ★★★

Keep it together for the run out between the second and third bolts. Shake it off and move when you're ready. The rough stuff starts midway and stays on you until the top. (FA John Payne 1995; 4 bolts)

☐ 5. DETOX MOUNTAIN   5.12A ★★★★★

Strictly an endurance hike. Sprint past sloped holds, multiple cruxes, and the occasional jug to reach the chains. Without a doubt the best of the grade in the canyon. (FA Rich Bechler 1990; 6 bolts)

"THE FARMER" and **"THE CARPENTER"** begin on the small ledge and share the first bolt.

☐ 6. THE FARMER   5.12A ★★★

See right.

☐ 7. THE CARPENTER   5.11A ★★★

Begin on **"THE FARMER"** and head right toward the flake feature. This route can be identified by the glue-in bolts that protect the face.

(FA Phillip Carrier and Jesse Koerner 2013; 7 bolts)

☐ 8. ODE TO MARY JOE   5.11A ★★★

This is the last bolted route on the wall just as the main cliff turns the corner toward the Minnow Area.

(FA Harry Gruszcyk & John Hein 1997; 6 bolts)

☐ **6. THE FARMER**   **5.12A** ★★★

Tie in and try to hold on long enough to power through the
short-lived crimp section at the top.

(FA Jim Thurmond 1990; 6 bolts)

Lauren Loesch on The Farmer 5.12a. Photo Phillip Carrier.

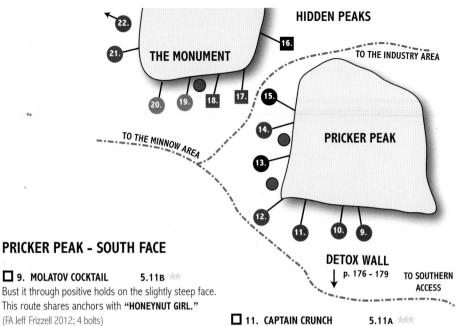

PRICKER PEAK - SOUTH FACE

☐ **9. MOLATOV COCKTAIL**   **5.11B** ★★
Bust it through positive holds on the slightly steep face.
This route shares anchors with **"HONEYNUT GIRL."**
(FA Jeff Frizzell 2012; 4 bolts)

☐ **10. HONEYNUT GIRL**   **5.11A** ★★★
Trickier and more challenging than the others on the wall;
this route begins above the large, flat rock near the base
of the boulder. (FA Jason Williams 1999; 4 bolts)

☐ **11. CAPTAIN CRUNCH**   **5.11A** ★★★
This route climbs the face directly to the right of **"CHEERIO
BOWL."** Often overlooked, this route is remarkably straight-
forward and features positive holds. Good for anyone
making the leap from pulling on plastic.
(FA Scott Swanson 1995; 5 bolts)

☐ 12. CHEERIO BOWL   5.10A ⭑⭑⭑⭑⭑

This route climbs the gently overhanging arête on the South face of Pricker Peak. Catch your breath at the no hands rest near the halfway point. Eventually talk yourself into leaving the security of your nest and climb the arête that hovers conspicuously above the break. Definitely an adventure!

(FA Eric Ulner 1993; 8 bolts)

John Payne on Cheerio Bowl 5.10a. Photo Matthew P. Guempel.

HIDDEN PEAKS

22.

21. **THE MONUMENT** **16.**

TO THE INDUSTRY AREA

20. **19.** **18.** **17.** **15.**

14. PRICKER PEAK

PRICKER PEAK - WEST FACE

13.

☐ **13. RAISIN BRAN**   **5.12c** ★★★★
Step around the corner from the **"CHEERIO BOWL"** arête
to locate the pocketed face. This amazing line features
back-to-back low percentage cruxes. Get organized at
the break and prepare to fight through the blank head
wall above. (FA Chris Schmick 2000; 6 bolts)

12.

11. **10.** **9.**

☐ **14. LUCKY CHARMS**   **5.11c** ★★★
Begin by climbing through fragile holds to gain the small
dihedral. After enjoying a short lived lay-back section,
punch through the shoulder-busting crux. This route
shares the last bolt and anchors of the previous line,
"RAISIN BRAN." It's way more fun than I'm making it
sound. (FA Eric Ulner 1993; 8 bolts)

DETOX WALL
p. 178 - 179

TO SOUTHERN
ACCESS

☐ **15. BETTER EAT YOUR WEEDIES 5.12b** ★★
Moderate climbing leads to the short, but technical crux on
marginal holds. (FA Chris Loesch 2004; 6 bolts)

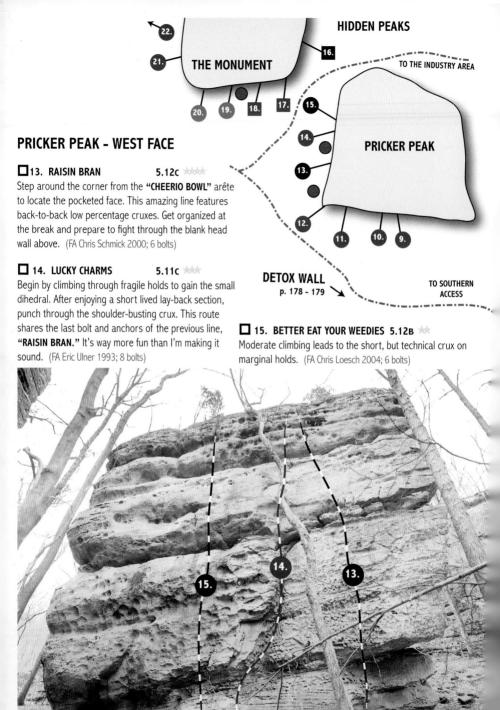

15. **14.** **13.**

THE MONUMENT - EAST FACE

The Southern face of The Monument has a variety of moderate mixed and sport routes. The Eastern face has two of the boulder's more serious lines: **"THE JUGGLER" 5.12A** and the classics **"NAKED BLADE" 5.11A**. Routes on The Monument are numbered from right to left.

☐ **16. THE JUGGLER**   **5.12A** ★★

Climb the massive and sweeping Northeast side of the Monument Boulder. Bolts protect the majority of the route, but you'll need some big gear to protect large layback section at the top.

(FA Eric Ulner 1995; Mixed: Gear + 5 bolts)

17.

16.

THE MONUMENT - SOUTH & WEST FACES

☐ **18. LOTHLORIEN**   5.10B

Easily identified by the large undercling flake above the first bolt, this route features a unique and challenging slab section. As with most climbs, this one is much easier for anyone with reasonable height.
(FA Kathy Ulner 1989; Mixed: 4 bolts + Gear)

☐ **19. THE MONUMENT**   5.9

Much like the other routes on this block, this route climbs through some of the best rock quality in Jackson Falls. Start left of the tree. (FA Unknown; 4 bolts)

☐ **20. STUBBORN SWEDE**   5.8

An unbelievably good ride with all the hallmarks of a 5-star climb. This route can be identified by the large and sweeping ramp feature.
(FA Jeff Frizzell & Eric Ulner 2004; 6 bolts)

☐ **21. ROAD TO SERFDOM**   5.10D

This route is located on the West face of the Monument. Pull on brittle stone to gain more bullet grips above.
(FA Jeff Frizzell 2012; 4 bolts)

BONER'S BOULDER

The Boner's Boulder is located down the trail and a bit down the hill from the Monument Boulder. When you see the boulder, head straight for it.

☐ **22. FEED ME**   5.11B

Hike through good holds and killer rests to reach the seemingly blank section. It seems blank because it absolutely is. Levitate or perform some wizardry to gain the holds that are in sight but out of reach. Finish with some feel good climbing to clip the anchors.
(FA Chris Schmick 2000; 7 bolts)

☐ **17. NAKED BLADE**   **5.11A**

This is the sharp, knife-like arête on the right-hand side of the Monument Boulder. Be advised, the route is protected by bolts until you reach the crown of the arête. The slab above does not have bolts, but can be protected with gear. Tri-cams work well. (FA Eric Ulner 1988; Mixed: 4 bolts + Gear)

Jacob Teal on Naked Blade 5.11a. Photo Yusuf Daneshyar.

p. 184. Jenni Grafton on Stubborn Swede 5.8. Photo Dan Brayack.

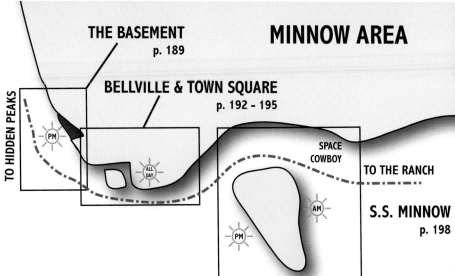

THE BASEMENT
p. 189

MINNOW AREA

BELLVILLE & TOWN SQUARE
p. 192 - 195

TO HIDDEN PEAKS

PM

ALL
DAY

SPACE
COWBOY

TO THE RANCH

AM

PM

S.S. MINNOW
p. 198

MINNOW AREA

The S.S. Minnow Area describes the bank of routes between Hidden Peaks and the Ranch. There are three distinct sections included in this area: The Basement, Bellville Wall/Town Square, and the S.S. Minnow boulder itself.

Given that each of these areas only offer a handful of routes, they have been combined under one heading.

APPROACH

Use the Southern Access point to reach Hidden Peaks. Hike through the Hidden Peaks corridor to rejoin the main trail that follows the cliffline Southwest. (A detailed description of this descent can be found on p. 31.)

The first area you will encounter is the Basement.

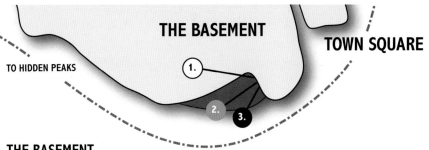

THE BASEMENT

The Basement is the short, but steep overhang encountered along the trail. Unfortunately, during the Spring this wall seeps constantly.

The king line here is without a doubt **"COUP D'ETAT"** **5.12D**. Keep this one at the top of your Fall/Winter tick list.

☐ 1. PROJECT

An undone line on the left side of the short, steep overhang. Wonder why there are no takers?   (3 bolts)

☐ 2. MISERY   5.13A ⭑⭑
The name says it all.
(FA Matt Bliss and Brian Capps 1995, 2 bolts)

☐ 2A. THE OBED SIMULATOR C 5.13C ⭑⭑
Begin on **"MISERY"** and head right toward **"COUP D'ETAT"** to link up with the same horizontal roof on **"THE OBED SIMULATOR B."** (FA John Flunker 2012; 7 bolts)

☐ 3. COUP D'ETAT   5.12D ⭑⭑⭑⭑
The plum line on the face. This route is the area's king line. Keep this one at the top of your Fall/Winter tick list. (FA Chris Schmick and Greg Thomas 1995; 9 bolts)

☐ 3A. THE OBED SIMULATOR B 5.13B ⭑⭑
Begin on **"COUP D'ETAT"**, grab a shake at the break and head left through the horizontal roof.
(FA John Flunker 2012; 8 bolts)

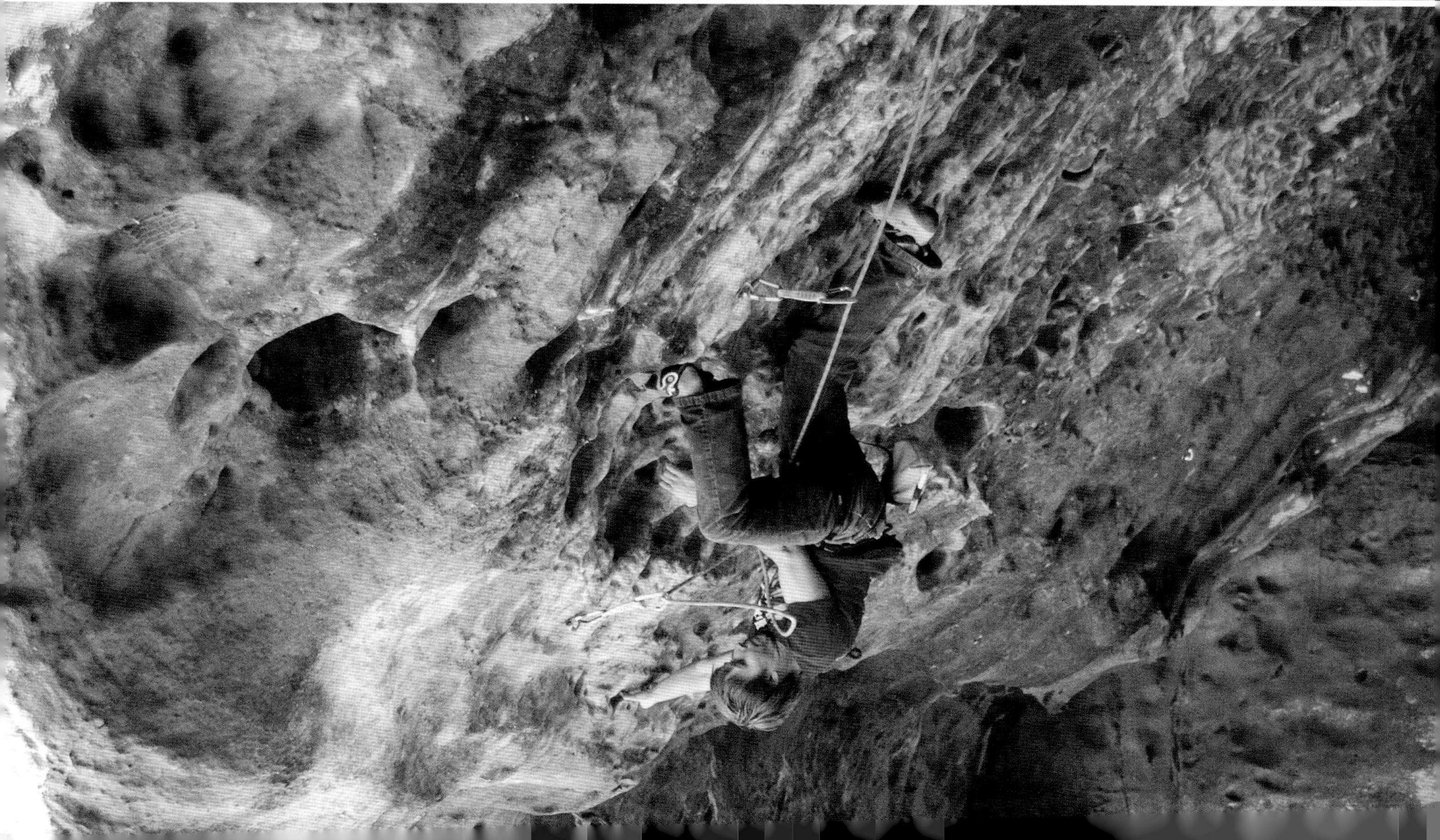

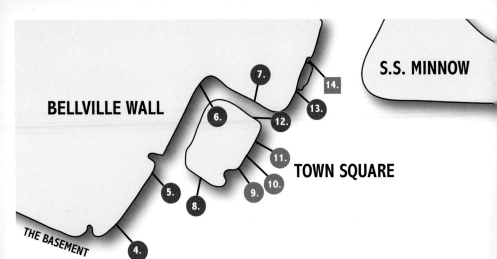

BELLVILLE WALL

S.S. MINNOW

TOWN SQUARE

THE BASEMENT

BELLVILLE WALL

Located around the corner from the Basement is a small boulder. There are a handful of moderate routes on the cliffline and on the boulder itself.

From the Basement, hike along the main trail and turn the corner. The first route on the main wall is route number 5, **"COURT HOUSE" 5.10B**.

☐ **4. COURT HOUSE**   **5.10B** ✮✮✮
This route is located South of the Basement where the cliff turns to make a rounded arête. Paddle through positive holds, clipping glue in bolts along the way.
(FA Chris Schmick 2001; 5 bolts)

☐ **5. LINDAPALOOZA**   **5.10D** ✮✮
Further down you will encounter this route at the entrance to the cave formed by the cliff and the large house-sized boulder. Kind of spooky back there!
(FA Jeff Allison and Jim Schneider 1998; 5 bolts)

☐ **6. UNCLE ALBERT PLAYS THE BLUES 5.11B** ✮✮
Even further down, the cliff turns sharply to form a dihedral. This route is located left of the large gully within the dihedral.
(FA Jim Schneider and Jeff Allison 1998; 5 bolts)

☐ **7. GULLY GEE WHIZ**   **5.10B** ✮✮✮
Before the main cliff turns the corner is this route with the prominent narrow gully between the second and third bolts. A lot like Robin Williams- pretty fun and kind of hairy. (FA Scott Mueller 1998; 4 bolts)

TOWN SQUARE

This small boulder has some cool short routes.

☐ **8. I BE LICHEN IT**   5.10B ☆☆
Currently, this is the only sport route on the North side of the Town Square Boulder. Climb the slight and continuous overhang. Really Fun! (FA Michael Lohrum 1998; 4 bolts)

☐ **9. MONKEY SHOWER**   5.9 ☆
This short line is on the West side of the Town Square Boulder, and directly right of the small gully that divides it.
(FA Jim Schneider, Margie Belt, Mike Braun 1998; 3 bolts)

☐ **10. KATIE DID**   5.9 ☆
Just right of the tree is another little guy.
(FA Jim Schneider, Margie Belt, Mike Braun 1998; 3 bolts)

☐ **11. SPANK YOU VERY MUCH**   5.9 ☆
Short. Not much else to say.
(FA Jeff Frizzell 2004; 5 bolts)

☐ **12. DANCES WITH SHARKS**   5.11B ☆☆
This route is located around the corner from the previous routes and cattycorner from **"GULLY GEE WHIZ."** Climb the dark and slightly overhanging face to gain the gully.
(FA Jeff Frizzell and Matt Queen 2013; 4 bolts)

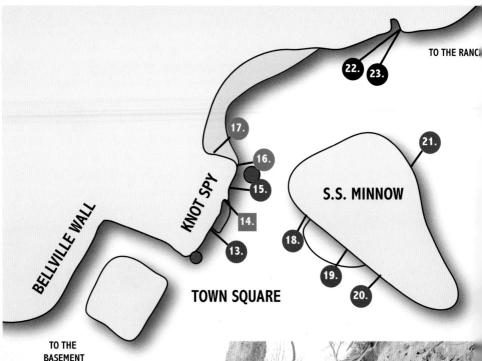

TO THE RANCH

S.S. MINNOW

KNOT SPY

BELLVILLE WALL

TOWN SQUARE

TO THE
BASEMENT

KNOT SPY

The next section includes the handful of routes past the Town Square Boulder and before and behind the S.S. Minnow Boulder.

☐ **13. UNKNOWN**   **5.10D** ★★
Just around the corner you will find the small boulder resting beneath the short, sparsely pocketed face. A difficult start gives way to a rousing game of find the underclings.   (FA Unknown; 3 bolts)

☐ **14. DOUBLE KNOT SPY**   **5.8** ★★★
This beautiful feature begs to be climbed. Worth doing for sure.   (FA Unknown; Gear)

☐ **15. BUBBLING CRUDE**   **5.10D** ★★
This is the bolted route 7 feet right of the obvious left-facing crack, **"DOUBLE KNOT SPY."**   Climbs up the rad face.   (FA Eric Miler 2013; 4 bolts)

☐ **16. POSSUM GRITS 5.9** ★★★
This one is located directly right of **"BUB-BLING CRUDE"** and just before the wall turns the corner. Reach the summit by sampling holds on the slab and the arête.
(FA Ed English 1998; 4 bolts)

☐ **17. WHEE DOGGIES! 5.8** ★★
At the base of the cliff is an in-set, triangular platform. You and your belayer will have to scramble to the top of this feature in order to begin the route. I'd like to think Jim chose the name because this thing is a really fun ride. Wheeeeeeee!
(FA Jim Schneider 2000; 4 bolts)

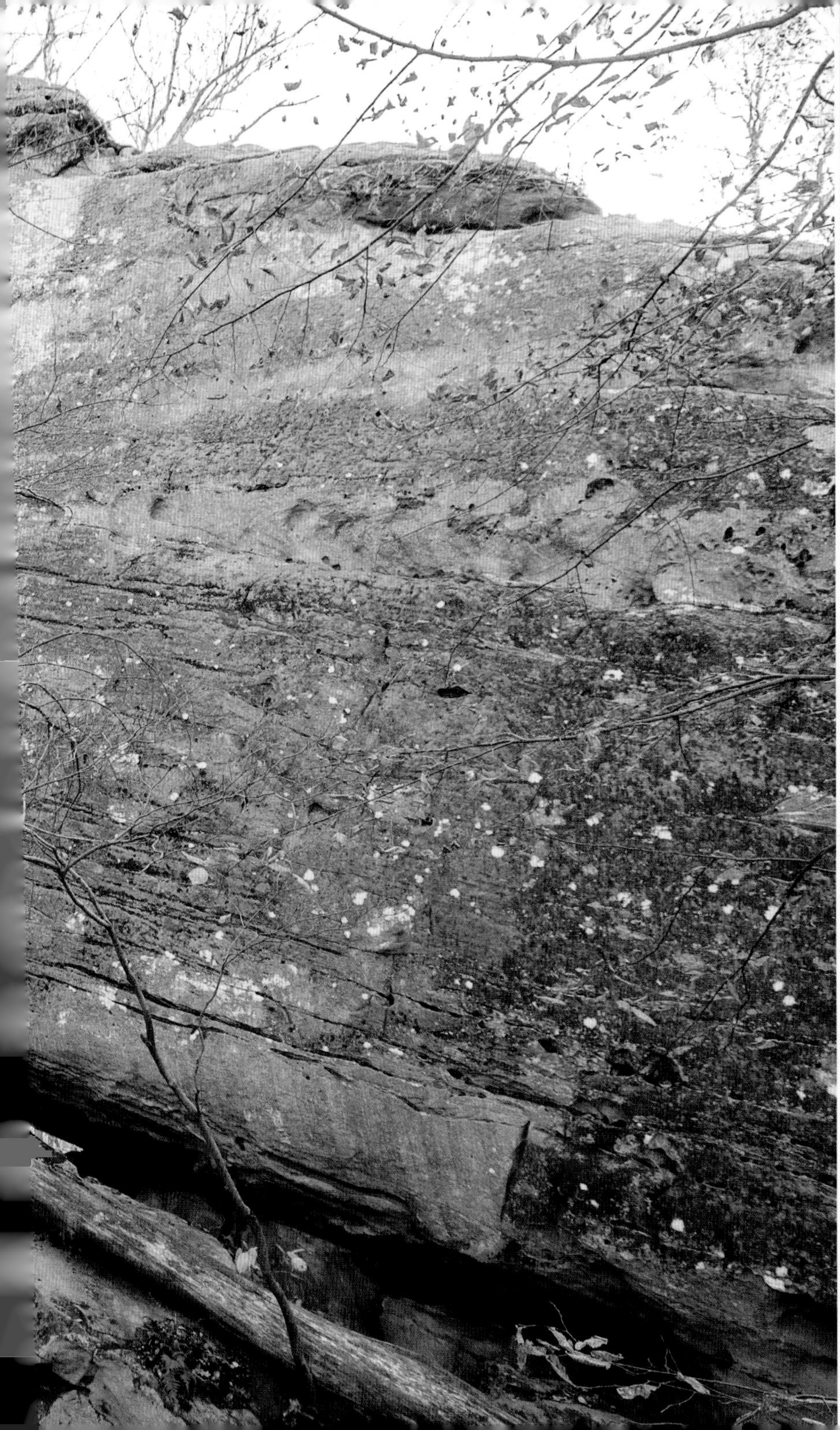

S.S. MINNOW

The S.S. Minnow boulder offers more challenging climbs than the previous areas and is worth the stop for the 5.10 climber. The climbs on the S.S. Minnow are a nail biters so make sure to stick clip the first or second bolt.

Step just around the corner from the Bellville Wall to locate the large ship-shaped boulder. The first route on the left side of the boulder is route number 18, **"THREE HOUR TOUR" 5.10B**.

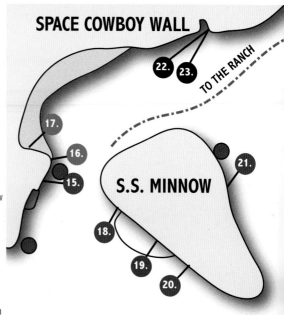

☐ **18. THREE HOUR TOUR 5.10B** ★★★★
This route is located on the North side of the S.S. Minnow and can be seen when approaching from Town Square. Climb leftward toward the rippling arête and turn the corner after the last bolt. Stay on the left side of the arête and on your game for the run at the top!
(FA Eric Ulner 1990; 5 bolts)

☐ **19. SWABBE**   **5.11A** ★★
This route climbs the middle of the boulder. Beneath this route is a collection of small boulders that you will need to climb up to reach the starting holds. Kind of treacherous.   (FA Jeff Frizzell 2013; 5 bolts)

☐ **20. SALTY DOG**   **5.10A** ★★★
This is the shortest and right most line on the North side of the Minnow Boulder. This route starts from the floor. (FA Jeff Frizzell 2013; 4 bolts)

☐ **21. SKIPPER**   **5.10B** ★★★
Located on the South side of the S.S. Minnow is one of the boulder's first additions since 1990. Climb rightward toward the arête using sinker holds. After gaining the face, tread lightly through tricky terrain. Leaning against the tree at the 2nd bolt is a difficult proposition to pass up. (FA Eric Miller 2013; 7 bolts)

☐ 22. SPACE COWBOY 5.12B

This route begins on the right side of the overhanging dihedral and climbs left onto the blank and beautiful face. I know what you're thinking and the answer is yes, there are holds up there. (FA Russell Rowlands 1995; 8 bolts)

☐ 23. GANGSTER OF LOVE 5.12C

This route is a variation to **"SPACE COWBOY."** After clipping the last bolt, continuing left to another set of anchors rather than heading straight up. Believe it or not, there are holds up there too! (FA Russell Rowlands 1995; 8 bolts)

p. 199. Kristi Ganz on Space Cowboy 5.12b. Photo Phillip Carrier, Kevin Sierzega Collection.

THE RANCH AREA

RANCH LEFT
p. 204 – 209

VERY
EARLY

ALL
DAY

RANCH RIGHT
p. 210 – 211

VERY
EARLY

ALL
DAY

TO THE MINNOW AREA

VISTA & COWBOY
p. 214 - 215

LA HACIENDA
p. 216 - 217

GENTLEMENS GROTTO
p. 218 - 219

VERY EARLY

ALL DAY

ALL DAY

THE RANCH AREA

The relatively long hike to the Ranch is well worth it. Don't let the angle turn you off! These routes have a different style than the other slabs at Jackson Falls.

Don't leave the canyon without trying **"GROOVY MAR-CIA" 5.9, "KILL BILL" 5.10A, "LASSO THE VULTURE" 5.11A,** and **"THRILL JILL" 5.12B.**

APPROACH

Use the Southern Access point to reach Hidden Peaks. Hike through the Hidden Peaks corridor to rejoin the main trail that follows the cliffline Southwest. (A detailed description of this descent can be found on p. 31.)

Continue past the S.S. Minnow boulder. A brief uphill will bring you to route number 1, **"LAND OF NOD" 5.10B.**

Hike downhill from **"LAND OF NOD"** and through the narrow corridor to reach a flat platform boulder. The first bolted route here is route number 3, **"BRIEF RESPITE" 5.8.**

RANCH AREA

THE RANCH

| 5.5 | 5.6 | 5.7 | 5.8 | 5.9 | 5.10 | 5.11 | 5.12 | 5.13 |

24 ROUTES

LA HACIENDA

| 5.5 | 5.6 | 5.7 | 5.8 | 5.9 | 5.10 | 5.11 | 5.12 | 5.13 |

10 ROUTES

GENTLMENS GROTTO

| 5.5 | 5.6 | 5.7 | 5.8 | 5.9 | 5.10 | 5.11 | 5.12 | 5.13 |

9 ROUTES

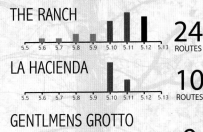

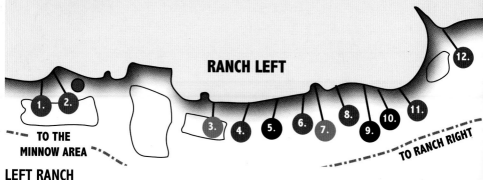

RANCH LEFT

TO THE
MINNOW AREA

TO RANCH RIGHT

LEFT RANCH
The "Left Ranch" includes routes 1 through 11.

☐ **1. THE LAND OF NOD**   **5.10B** ☆☆
Aptly named; this route is located in the undeveloped section of the cliff between the S.S. Minnow Boulder and the Ranch. A challenging start on dark stone gives way to spectacular and more featured climbing above.
(FA Jeff Frizzell 2004; 6 bolts)

☐ **2. MAD HATTER**   **5.10C** ☆☆
Directly right of **"LAND OF THE NOD"** is this left-angling line that moves over orange stone. (FA Jeff Frizzell 2004; 4 bolts)

☐ **3. BRIEF RESPITE**   **5.8** ☆☆☆☆
This is the first bolted route encountered after hiking up and then downhill along the cliffline and is directly across from the large, flat boulder. Scramble up the slab near the large gully clipping bolts along the way.
(FA Eric Ulner & David Hart 1995; 6 bolts)

☐ **4. ROCKET MORTON**   **5.11C** ☆☆
This route is a recent addition to cliff and an instant classic. Incredibly varied climbing through pockets and slopers comes to a halt at the final push for the anchors. Don't forget to breathe! (FA Jeff Frizzell 2013; 5 bolts)

☐ **5. EVER READY BETTY**   **5.12A** ☆☆☆☆
Wow. Really hard would be putting it mildly. Begin by negotiating the thin and almost featureless slab by utilizing a combination of wizardry and wishful thinking. Keep your guard up; the climbing after the first bolt doesn't let up until you clip the chains. You'll earn your points on this one for sure.
(FA Jeff Frizzell 2004; 5 bolts)

☐ **6. MIRROR MAN**   **5.11C** ☆☆☆
A LOT tougher than it looks. Resist the urge to climb toward the gully in search of better holds.
(FA Jeff Frizzell 2004; 5 bolts)

Allison Moran on Land of Nod 5.10b. Photo Kevin Sierzega.

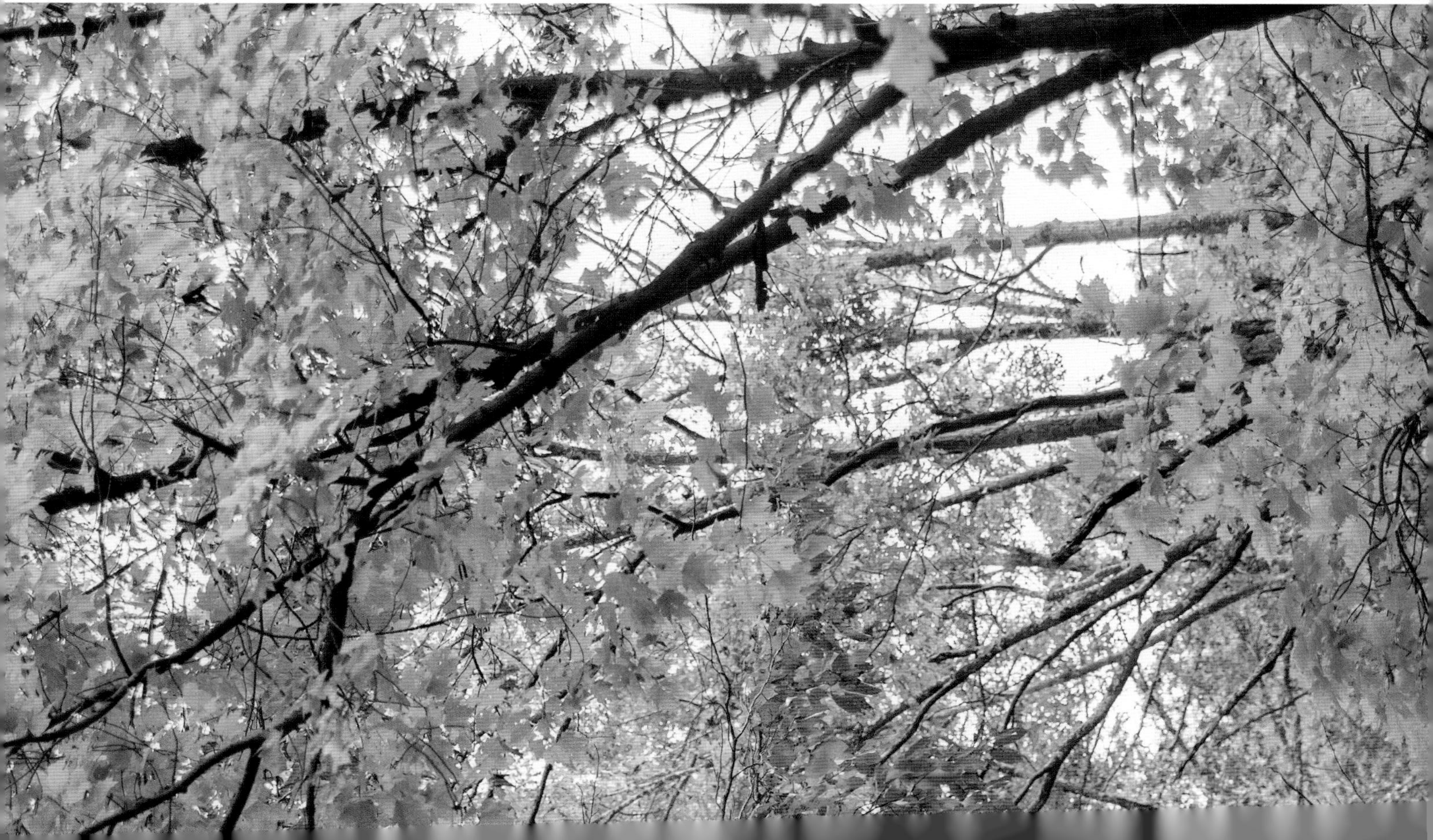

Phillip Carrier on Disco Fever 5.12c. Photo Kevin Sierzega.

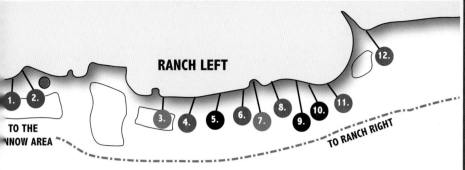

RANCH LEFT

1. 2.

TO THE
INNOW AREA

3. 4. 5. 6. 7. 8. 9. 10. 11. 12.

TO RANCH RIGHT

☐ **7. GROOVY MARCIA**   **5.9** ★★★★
A spectacular and unique geological feature. Press, stem, beg, and plead your way up the large water groove in the middle of the wall. This feature was formed primarily by water erosion and often stays wet for days after a decent rain. If you catch it dry don't pass it up! (FA Eric Ulner 1995; 6 bolts)

☐ **8. COWGIRLS IN THE SAND**   **5.11B** ★★★
This route begins on **"GROOVY MARCIA"** and shares the first bolt. Climb through the gully and reach out right to clip the second bolt. Take a deep breath, step on to the face and crimp hard on your way to the chains. (FA Jeff Frizzell 2004; 7 bolts)

☐ **9. DISCO FEVER**   **5.12c** ★★★
See left.

☐ **10. URSA MINOR**   **5.12D** ★★★
Pull hard between sinker pockets to reach the unique and challenging crux at the halfway point.
(FA Jared Smith 2014; 7 bolts)

☐ **11. LASSO THE VULTURE**   **5.11A** ★★★★★
Use the braille method to discover the hidden holds that lead to the large gully near the top of the route. Who said there's no adventure in sport climbing?
(FA Eric Ulner, Kathy Ulner, & John Sommerhof 1994; 7 bolts)

☐ **12. CONDOR**   **5.11c**
Climb the arête to the right of the large gully.
(FA Russell Rowlands 1995; 5 bolts)

☐ **13. THRILL JILL**   **5.12b**
This brilliant route climbs through the right-angling
seam around the corner from the **"CONDOR"** arête.
Keep it together as you climb through sloping huecos and the occasional pocket by power smearing
your feet. Regain your composure before you launch
into the heart breaker crux that protects the chains.
One of my personal favorites.
(FA Jeff Frizzell 2004; 5 bolts)

☐ **14. LITTLE BLUE PILL**   **5.11b**
Start to the right of the tree and power smear or
high step to gain what few holds exist on the face.
Keep your eye out for the peanut hold; it's a life-
saver! (FA Jeff Frizzell 2013; 6 bolts)

☐ **15. KILL BILL**   **5.10a**
This one starts just before going up the small hill. One
of the best 5.10s at Jackson Falls. Patiently make your
way up the short but demanding slab. Reach the summit
by climbing above the anchors and take in the view.
This route shares anchors with **"BENNY HILL."** (FA Bill
Ritchie 2004; 4 bolts)

☐ **16. BENNY HILL**   **5.10c**
This is the last route on the wall where the ground
begins to slope uphill. Climb the sparsely pocketed face
and tread lightly on your wait to the anchors. Shares
anchors with **"KILL BILL."** (FA Jeff Frizzell 2013; 4 bolts)

☐ **17. SOUTHERN INQUISITION 5.10b**
This route is located on the large, steep boulder-like
protrusion on the left side of the trail prior to the Vista
Wall. It is the only bolted route on the Southeast face of
this feature. (FA Russell Rowlands 1995; 5 bolts)

p. 211. Billy Budd on Kill Bill 5.10a. Photo Kevin Sierzega.

So iLL

WWW.SOILLHOLDS.COM

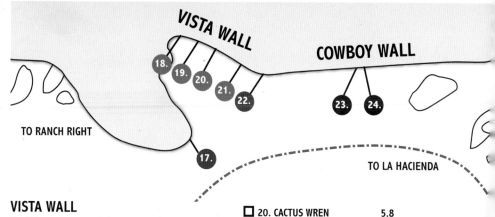

VISTA WALL

Uphill from **"SOUTHERN INQUISITION"** (p. 211) the cliffline continues. A band of short, deep red stone houses the following routes. Near the dihedral and on the far left side of the low angle slab is the first route.

☐ **18. FRONT PORCH VISTA** 5.7 ★★★
This route is located left of the small tree in front of the wall. (FA Jeff Frizzell 2013)

☐ **19. CLOUD SHADOW** 5.6
Just right of the tree, this route climbs through the dark red water groove. (FA Jeff Frizzell 2013)

☐ **20. CACTUS WREN** 5.8
This route shares anchors with **"CLOUD SHADOW."**
(FA Jeff Frizzell 2013)

☐ **21. ROAD RUNNER** 5.9
Clip the first bolt on **"CACTUS WREN"** and move right.
(FA Jeff Frizzell 2013)

☐ **22. CARA CARA** 5.11c
This route begins slightly downhill from the previous lines. Climb the short arête to reach a brief encounter with the overhanging bulge. This line shares anchors with **"ROAD RUNNER."** (FA Jeff Frizzell 2013)

Ben Wun on Cowboys and Cross Dressers 5.12a. Photo Matt Maxwell.

☐ **23. COWBOYS AND CROSS DRESSERS 5.12A** ✦✦✦✦
The only thing keeping this one from getting 5 stars is the height, but don't let that stop you from tying in. Hike through the rainbow-streaked wall using pockets, edges and the occasional sinker hold.
(FA Russell Rowlands 1995; 4 bolts)

☐ **24. DARWIN'S THEORY**   **5.12B** ✦✦✦
Climb the right-angling undercling feature to gain the gently overhanging face. Tic-tac through thin holds or just take the good ones by moving dynamically.
(FA Russell Rowlands 1995; 4 bolts)

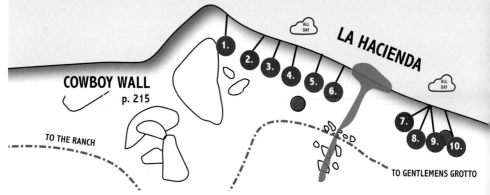

LA HACIENDA AREA

La Hacidenda is located just beyond the Ranch. This wall receives little sunlight and provides some relief for climbers looking to beat the heat in the warmer months.

APPROACH

Continue past the Ranch area until the trail begins to head slightly downhill. A small boulder rests on the right hand side of the trail at the bottom of the slope.

The route directly left of the dark water streak is number 6, **"BAD HOMBRE" 5.11A**.

☐ **1. TWISTED GOAT**   5.10D ★★★★
This route climbs the unique, shallow gully on the left-hand side of the wall. Climb through amazing pockets to reach a tough undercling move. Expect some challenging positions. (FA Jeff Frizzell 2013; 4 bolts)

☐ **2. BUCKAROO**   5.11A ★★★
Fire through good pockets until they run out. Press your luck to find the one good hold left and finish on easier climbing to the chains. (FA Jeff Frizzell 2013; 4 bolts)

☐ **3. BARBED WIRE**   5.10D ★★★
Inch your way up on pale holds to gain the hueco near the 4th bolt where things let up considerably. (FA Jeff Frizzell 2013; 4 bolts)

☐ **4. JAVELINA**   5.10D ★★★
This route begins on the coarse and heavily featured horizontal break near the waterfall. Climb through the two large huecos and find the knee bar near the halfway point to take the edge off before heading into the pocket crux above. This routes shares anchors with **"HIGH LONE-SOME."** (FA Jeff Frizzell 2013; 4 bolts)

☐ **5. HIGH LONESOME**   5.10D ★★
This route shares anchors with **"JAVELINA."** Climb straight up the face. (FA Jeff Frizzell 2013; 4 bolts)

☐ **6. BAD HOMBRE**   5.11A ★★
This route is directly left of the large waterfall in the center of the cliff. Spray from the waterfall often makes the first few holds damp. This route stops just short of the top. (FA Jeff Frizzell 2013; 4 bolts)

Directly right of the waterfall are 3 routes that share the same first bolt.

☐ **7. SIERRA NEGRO**   5.11A ★★
Climb leftward to reach the second bolt and continue heading left to clip the third and furthest line of bolts. Finish by climbing straight up through the blunt layback feature. (FA Jeff Frizzell 2013; 4 bolts)

☐ **8. BLACK EYED BEAUTY**   5.10D ★★
As with the previous route, bear left after clipping the first bolt to head toward the second. Continue climbing leftward until you encounter the middle line of bolts. (FA Jeff Frizzell 2013; 4 bolts)

☐ **9. THREE AMIGOS**   5.10D ★★
This route shares the start with **"BLACK EYED BEAUTY"** but heads straight up from the first bolt which these three routes share. (FA Jeff Frizzell 2013; 4 bolts)

☐ **10. PONCHO VILLA**   5.10A ★★
On the right hand side is the last route in the area and the only independent line on the wall. Climb through the iron plated face. (FA Jeff Frizzell 2013; 4 bolts)

GENTLEMENS GROTTO

The Gentlemen's Grotto is located in the Southern-most part of the canyon and is the last area with established and bolted routes. This area has been growing steadily thanks to enterprising individuals with rotary hammer drills.

With the exception of **"GENTLEMEN PREFER NATURE GIRLS"** **5.12c**, most of the routes are short and dead vertical.

APPROACH

Use the Southern Access point to reach Hidden Peaks. Hike through the Hidden Peaks corridor to rejoin the main trail that follows the cliffline Southwest.

Continue past La Hacienda until the trail begins to head slightly downhill. A small boulder rests on the right hand side of the trail at the bottom of the slope.

GENTLEMENS GROTTO

1. 2. 3. 4.

TOP HAT TOWER

TO LA HACIENDA

5.
6.
7.
9.
8.

TOP HAT TOWER

☐ **1. BLACK TIE AFFAIR**   **5.11D** ⋆⋆

This route features sustained climbing through huecos and edges and finishes with an exciting layback section. (FA Chris Gottlieb and Kevin La Forge 2013; 3 bolts)

☐ **2. BOW TIE AND BILLFOLD**   **5.12A** ⋆

A tough lock-off right off the ground leads to great climbing above. (FA Chris Gottlieb and Kevin La Forge 2013; 3 bolts)

☐ **3. HARDWOOD HABERDASHER 5.10A** ⋆⋆⋆

One of the Grotto's best. A powerful start leads to the heavily featured bulge. Turn the lip and tread carefully on your way to the anchors. (FA Chris Gottlieb and Kevin La Forge 2013; 3 bolts)

☐ **4. TUX WITH TAILS**   **5.8** ⋆

On the right side of the left-leaning chimney is the last bolted route on the main cliff. Climbing on positive holds lead to the series of iron flakes. (FA Chris Gottlieb and Kevin La Forge 2013; 2 bolts)

☐ **5. CIGARS AND SCOTCH**   **5.7** ⋆⋆

Follow the right side of the arête on good pockets and underclings. (FA Chris Gottlieb and Kevin La Forge 2013; 3 bolts)

☐ **6. OWL-CAT**   **5.10D** ⋆⋆

Pull through sustained tricky moves. (FA Chris Gottlieb and Kevin La Forge 2013; 3 bolts)

☐ **7. KRAKENDILE**   **5.10C** ⋆

Start a little left and work a move using positive, yet hidden holds. Cruise easier terrain to the finish. (FA Chris Gottlieb and Kevin La Forge 2013; 3 bolts)

☐ **8. TOP HAT AND CANE**   **5.11C** ⋆⋆⋆

A short face leads to a beefy roof with big moves on decent holds. (FA Chris Gottlieb and Kevin La Forge 2013; 3 bolts)

☐ **9. GENTLEMEN PREFER NATURE GIRLS 5.12C** ⋆⋆⋆

Take on the burly roof using heelhooks, kneebars, and brute strength. (FA Kevin Sierzega and Phillip Carrier 2013; 3 bolts)

Kevin Sierzega on Gentlemen Prefer Nature Girls 5.12c. Photo Kevin Sierzega.

PROMISED LAND OVERVIEW

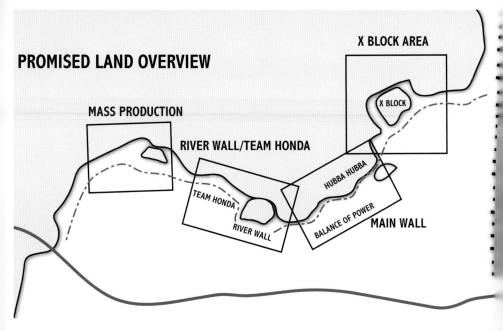

X BLOCK AREA

X BLOCK

MASS PRODUCTION

RIVER WALL/TEAM HONDA

TEAM HONDA

RIVER WALL

HUBBA HUBBA

BALANCE OF POWER

MAIN WALL

THE PROMISED LAND

The Promised Land is essentially one main wall and several boulders. This map shows the general location of each of the areas, though each area flows right into the next. On p. 223, these are further broken into specific walls.

This section is numbered from right to left; the order encountered from the approach.

PROMISED LAND

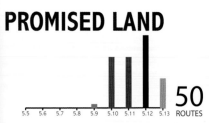

50 ROUTES

p. 234. John Flunker on Circle in the Round 5.13b. Photo Chris Loesch.

PHILLIP CARRIER

Phillip Carrier's story begins with his father's. In the early 1980s, Alan Carrier was at the forefront of the climbing movement in Southern Illinois. Climbing was slowly making its transition from natural to fixed protection and the physical boundaries of the sport were being challenged. Alan was one of the few Americans at the time to climb the grade of 5.12.

Prior to the information age and the rise of the indoor climbing gym, the practice of climbing was strictly an oral tradition. Learned skills and personal experiences were the products of mentorship and personal guidance.

Alan shared his experience and passion for climbing with Phillip early on. As Phillip matured, so did his appreciation for the sport. It gave them something in common. "I feel lucky to have him be the one that took me climbing and who showed me Jackson Falls. My climbing partner was my dad, a person who helped develop the area."

Having spent years walking the length of the canyon with his father, Philip began to see potential in many of Jackson Falls' untouched faces. In 2006, Phillip picked up a hammer drill for the first time and bolted four routes at the Applejack Wall. Consumed by the excitement of discovering new lines, Phillip spent hours hanging on a rope in the middle of the night that winter. "I felt like I had to. I didn't want to do anything else. I bolted most of them at night because I wanted to climb in the morning."

What started as a creative expression of his climbing experience evolved into a passion to provide opportunities for others. "I wanted other climbers to see these routes. I wanted to share my experience and routes with other people." Phillip bolted nearly 20 routes in the canyon that year, many of them in the grade of 5.11. "I spent my time and energy at Jackson Falls because I have an intimate and personal relationship with the area, and because I care so much about it."

Phillip has helped to maintain the area's longstanding "Keep Jackson Stainless" initiative. The program encouraged developers to only use stainless steel protection when establishing and re-bolting routes. Stainless steel bolts are far more resilient to corrosion than other materials. This practice ensured that fixed protection in the canyon would last longer. "It is important to think past the first ascent. I want to make sure that the routes I bolt are safe for others to enjoy decades later."

Beyond creating more opportunities for individuals to enjoy Jackson Falls, Phillip Carrier represents what climbing should be: an experience that can be enriched when shared with people.

Photos Top: Yusuf Daneshyar, Right: Matthew P. Guempel.

NOTABLE
FIRST ASCENTS

p.234. Aaron Stover on Pool of Reflection 5.13b. Photo Dan Brayack.

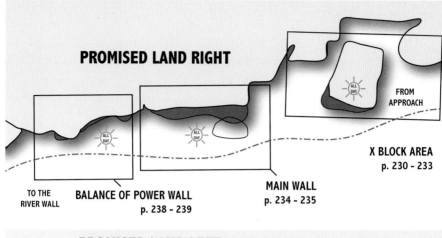

PROMISED LAND RIGHT

FROM APPROACH

X BLOCK AREA
p. 230 - 233

TO THE RIVER WALL

BALANCE OF POWER WALL
p. 238 - 239

MAIN WALL
p. 234 - 235

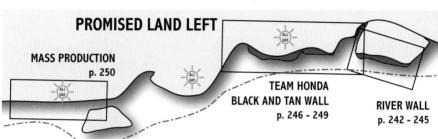

PROMISED LAND LEFT

MASS PRODUCTION
p. 250

TEAM HONDA
BLACK AND TAN WALL
p. 246 - 249

RIVER WALL
p. 242 - 245

PROMISED LAND

The Promised Land was discovered in the late 1990s by Chris Schmick and Russell Rowlands. This satellite area is part of a smaller hollow Southwest of the main Jackson Falls hollow. The aptly name Promised Land is a superior area for strong sport climbers. Come equipped with some serious try-hard and a strong fitness game. Most the routes here range in difficulty from 5.12b to 5.13b, but there are a handful of moderates worth checking out; namely **"FOUR BETTYS" 5.10D**, **"BETTER LATE THAN NEVER" 5.11C**, and **"TACO'S ATV JAMBOREE" 5.11D**.

The Promised Land is almost entirely South-facing and stays I the sun all day. This is THE place to climb in colder months, but is absolutely brutal during the summer.

PROMISED LAND APPROACH MAP

RAILROAD ROCK

NORTH CANYON
p. 32 - 72

NORTH FALLS
p. 112 - 155

Glen Street Falls Road

HOBO CAVE

GALLERY

WEST FALLS
p. 74 - 111

BIG STAR WALL

BATTLE AXE

LOVELY TOWER

BEAVER WALL

RAINY DAY ROOF

MR. JIMMY BOULDER

DOG WALK ACCESS

2.

HIDDEN PEAKS

EAST FALLS
p. 156 - 165

1.

BONER BOULDER

CREEK CROSSING

3.

4.

TOWN SQUARE

SOUTHERN ACCESS

PROMISED LAND
p. 220 - 250

S.S. MINNOW

SOUTH CANYON
p. 166 - 219

THE RANCH

X BLOCK

GENTLEMENS GROTTO

p. 234. Kevin Todd on Duppy Conqueror 5.12d. Photo Yusuf Daneshyar.

CONSIDERATIONS

The approach to the Promised Land can be challenging for the first time visitor. For that reason, I would strongly suggest using a compass in conjunction with the written directions and images provided. For a good visual idea, check out the map on p. 124.

Although these directions will keep you on Shawnee National Forest property and on foot trails designated by the Forest Service for the majority of the approach, you will need to cross the railroad tracks to access the sole trailhead for the Promised Land. Be advised that these tracks are the property of the Illinois Central Railroad. Please know that by being on the railroad tracks, you are assuming personal risk. That being said, by following these directions closely, you can significantly reduce the amount of time spent on the tracks.

APPROACH

(1) Make your way to the Dog Walk Access (see p. 31.)

(2) Continue hiking past the Dog Walk along the top trail for about 2000 feet. At this point you will encounter a large, flaring ravine (**Photo 2**) which is the Southern Access. Hike downhill through the ravine in order to reach the Hidden Peaks Area.

(3) Hike downhill toward the Monument Boulder (**Photo 3**) and locate the foot trail. Bear left to continue hiking Southwest until you see the large free-standing boulder downhill from the trail. This is Boner's Boulder.

(4) Make your way to Boner's Boulder (**Photo 4A**) and locate the route **"FEED ME" 5.11B**. Currently, this is the only bolted route on the boulder. Head straight downhill (no marked trail) to meet up with National Forest Trail 49D (**Photo 4B.**)

(5) Turn left and briefly hike Southwest until you reach the narrow stream that slopes downhill. Turn right (**Photo 5**) and head downhill to meet back with foot trail 49.

4B.

(6) Hike roughly 500 feet to reach the small creek. This is the first of four creek crossings. Cross the creek here (**Photo 6**) and meet up with the trail on the other side. This is trail number 49E. Turn left and hike Northwest along trail 49E.

(7) After hiking approximately 500 feet you will reach a steeper, but much shorter downhill slope. Turn left here (**Photo 7**) and head downhill toward Little Bay Creek where you will cross for a second time.

(8) After crossing the creek you will rejoin trail 49. Turn left and hike South. After roughly 500 feet the dirt foot trail will give way to the distinct sandy path that leads back to the creek. Cross the creek here for the third time and rejoin trail 49.

(9) Hike briefly uphill toward the small hallway formed by two small boulders (**Photo 9.**) The trail will bear right and head downhill toward the creek. Cross the creek here for the fourth and last time.

(10) Once you have made your way across the creek, make a left and continue South along the foot trail. Along the way you will encounter the boulder pictured below (**Photo 10.**)

5.

6.

7.

9.

10.

(11) After roughly 500 feet, a small collection of boulders will appear on the right side of the trail and uphill. A faint path leads up to these boulders. (If you hike too far, you will reach another creek crossing. Do not cross the creek again. Turn back and look for the path.)

(12) Follow this path uphill and hike leftward along the short cliff band pictured to the right (**Photo 12.**)

(13) The trail will eventually take you through the wide corridor formed by boulders on either side (**Photo 13.**)

(14) As the hill steepens, you will encounter a fence and a sign indicating the property boundaries of the National Forest (**Photos 14 and 14A.**)

(15) Continue hiking uphill until you reach the railroad tracks. Make a left and briefly head South.

(16) Cattycorner from where you hiked up you should see a series of cairns (**Photo 16**.) Cross the tracks here to find the trailhead leading up to the Promised Land.

(17) Hike uphill using the foot trail until you see the small boulder. This foot trail is designated as trail 001T.

(18) Hike West for another one tenth of a mile until you see the steep overhanging face and corridor pictured right. This is the X-Block (**Photo 17.**)

16.

17.

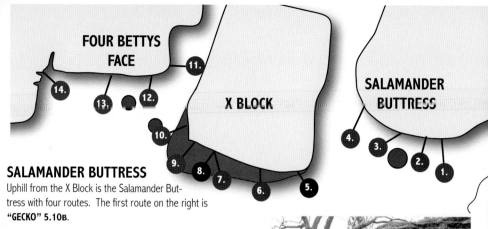

SALAMANDER BUTTRESS

Uphill from the X Block is the Salamander Buttress with four routes. The first route on the right is **"GECKO" 5.10B.**

☐ **1. SALAMANDER** 5.10C
This is the right-most route on the tower and shares anchors with **"CHAMELEON."** Start on the right side of the small talus boulder. (FA Chris Schmick 1998; 5 bolts)

☐ **2. CHAMELEON** 5.11B
Located just left of **"SALAMANDER"**, this one comes out swinging with a healthy low crux. Manage to tag the large side-pulling hueco and paddle through miserable holds to the shared anchors. Start on the middle of the small talus boulder. (FA Eric Heuermann 1998; 6 bolts)

☐ **3. SKINK** 5.10D
Start in front of the tree then move left at the second bolt. Climb over the bulge to anchors. (FA Chris Schmick 1998; 7 bolts)

☐ **4. GECKO** 5.10B
This is the first route on the left side of the buttress and ascends the rippling and pocketed face.
(FA Chris Schmick 1998; 6 bolts)

X BLOCK

☐ **5. XTERMINATOR** 5.12A
This is the right-most line on the South face of the X Block and climbs the arête feature. (FA Russell Rowlands 1998; 6 bolts)

☐ **6. X FACTOR** 5.11C
Similar in character to **"GENERATOR X"**, but a step down in terms of quality. (FA Chris Schmick 1998; 6 bolts)

☐ **7. GENERATOR X** 5.11C
Start five feet right of the arête. Pull on incut edges and jugs on the white washed face. Shake it off and bust through steep stone to reach the anchors. (FA Chris Schmick 1998; 6 bolts)

☐ **8. X-PECTING** 5.12B
This route begins on **"GENERATOR X"** but breaks left at the 5th bolt and heads through steeper terrain.
(FA Jesse Koerner 2012; 6 bolts)

☐ **9. XXX** 5.10A
This route starts on the left side of the main face of the X Block. Clip the two bolts on the right side of the arête and head left to join up with **"XOXO."**
(FA John Flunker 2008; 6 bolts)

☐ **10. XOXO** 5.10B
Climb the heavily featured and slightly overhanging West side of the X Block. (FA Russell Rowlands 1998; 7 bolts)

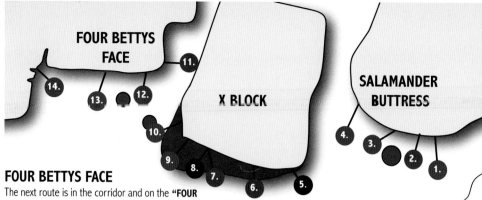

FOUR BETTYS FACE

The next route is in the corridor and on the **"FOUR BETTYS"** face. The routes continue around the face, numbered right to left.

☐ 11. THREE DAY IMPRESSION 5.11B ★★
Start just right of the arête around the corner from the main face. After the no-hands rest, tackle the flaring crack. (FA John Flunker 2008; 8 bolts)

☐ 12. TACO'S ATV JAMBOREE 5.11D ★★★★
See right.

☐ 13. FOUR BETTYS 5.10D ★★★★
This short but stellar face climb is located 15 feet right of the large wandering crack. Zig-zag between sloping huecos and pockets. Stay sharp at the third bolt; you have a 50/50 shot here, so choose wisely! (FA Chris Schmick 1998; 5 bolts)

☐ 14. CHOCOLATE PLATED 5.10C ★★★
Start left of the wide crack and follow the line of bolts up the plated face. (FA John Flunker 2008; 7 bolts)

☐ **12. TACO'S ATV JAMBOREE** **5.11D** ★★★★
Start 5 feet right of the tree. Climb the tricky face that
keeps you on your toes the whole way!
(FA John Flunker 2007; 6 bolts)

John Flunker on Taco's ATV Jamboree 5.11d. Photo Chris Loesch.

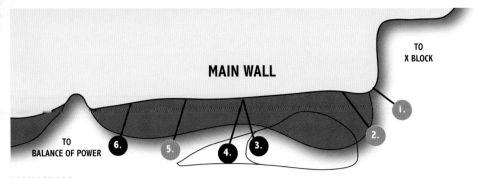

MAIN WALL

☐ **1. DROP OF REFLECTION   5.13A** ★★★★
This variation of the original line, **"POOL OF REFLEC-
TION,"** begins on the left-angling arête and joins it
at the 4th bolt. (FA John Flunker 2008; 10 bolts)

☐ **2. POOL OF REFLECTION   5.13B** ★★★★
This is the direct line on the overhanging face. A
low and severe crux on poor holds finishes with a
rough endurance haul to the top. It's a heartbreaker up there. (FA John Flunker 2010; 9 bolts)

☐ **3. HUBBA HUBBA   5.12D** ★★★★
Rock climbing doesn't get better than this. A must
do for the 5.12 climber. Begin on **"OOH LA LA"** and
break right after clipping the 4th bolt.
(FA Russell Rowlands 1998; 7 bolts)

☐ **4. OOH LA LA   5.12D** ★★★★
This route shares its start with **"HUBBA HUBBA"**
but follows the proud line straight up through the
prominent red streak.
(FA Russell Rowlands 1998; 6 bolts)

☐ **5. CIRCLE IN THE ROUND   5.13B** ★★★
Start 20 feet right of the dihedral and in front of
the end of the pation/view boulder. Go h.a.m. to
get through the boulder problem down low and
keep hustling as you make your way up the sustained headwall. (FA John Flunker 2007; 7 bolts)

☐ **6. DUPPY CONQUEROR   5.12D** ★★★★
Just right of the dihedral is the left-most bolted line
on the main wall. This one rips through the golden
streaked face on sculpted holds. Expect to encounter some standard sandstone deception near the
top. (FA Chris Loesch 2009; bolts)

p. 248. The Namesake for Trapline. Photo Dan Brayack.

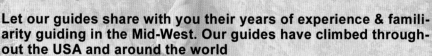

p. 234. John Flunker on Pool of Reflection 5.13b. Photo Chris Loesch.

HUBBA HUBBA

BALANCE OF POWER

TO CONGO SPRAY

BALANCE OF POWER

☐ **1. KEY LIME   5.11A** ✲
This route can be identified by the vibrant lime-green streak roughly 15 feet off the ground and near the large gully. Climb leftward on the face above the short bulging feature.
(FA John Flunker 2008; 5 bolts)

☐ **2. JARRED'S ROUTE 5.12A** ✲✲✲
Look for the glue in bolts that protect the bulging face. After making it through the short vertical section, pull through the horizontal roof and haul up the face.
(FA Jared Smith 2014; 5 bolts)

☐ **3. REMOVE LA ROPA 5.12B** ✲✲✲✲
Climb the left-angling line of bolts through the low, three-tiered roof. This is the area's obligatory horizontal roof.
(FA Chris Schmick 1998; 7 bolts)

☐ **4. ESSENCE OF POWER 5.12C** ✲✲✲✲
Battle the pump as you pull between sloping huecos on the red and golden streaked wall. Aid to the first bolt and finish on the 7th bolt.
(FA Chris Schmick 1998; 7 bolts)

☐ 5. BALANCE OF POWER   5.12c

The definitive five star climb: a solid Southern Illinois showcase complete with breathtaking aesthetics, incredible movement, and good height. This route is the single best reason to make the trek to the Promised Land. (FA Russell Rowlands 1998; 7 bolts)

☐ 6. MYSTICAL SEASON 5.13A

Begin on the large boulder beneath the roof on the left-most part of the wall. Grab the first set of holds and get ready to pull hard to gain the face that follows the arcing line of bolts.
(FA John Flunker 2010; 7 bolts)

Calvin Hwang on Balance of Power 5.12c. Photo Yolanda Chen.

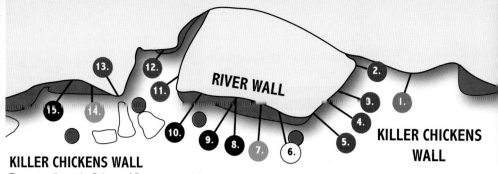

KILLER CHICKENS WALL

The next wall past the Balance of Power area contains a small collection of moderates. This is the Killer Chickens Wall. Continue around the corner to find the impressive River Wall.

☐ **1. VICTORIA'S SECRET**   **5.9** ⭐⭐

This route is located on the right side of the wall before the boulder and climbs through the prominent dark streak on the slab. The first bolt is quite high, and the risk of a rough landing exists if you blow it at the second. Despite the danger zone, it's definitely a fun romp worth checking out! (FA John Flunker, 4 bolts)

☐ **2. DELIRIOUS**   **5.10A** ⭐

The most accessible line on the wall, **"DELIRIOUS"** climbs the arête near the large chimney.
(FA Shawn Watson 1998, 3 bolts)

☐ **3. SPECTATOR SPORT**   **5.10A** ⭐⭐

You may need to bushwhack to find the start of this pocketed face climb. (FA Shawn Watson 1998, 4 bolts)

☐ **4. TRAFFIC JAM**   **5.10B** ⭐⭐

Fun climbing on good holds.
(FA Shawn Watson 1998, 5 bolts)

☐ **5. KILLER CHICKENS**   **5.11A** ⭐⭐⭐

This route is the line of bolts closest to the arête on the left-hand side of the wall. Follow the left-facing flake for for a bit, then move right over the bulge.
(FA Shawn Watson 1998; 5 bolts)

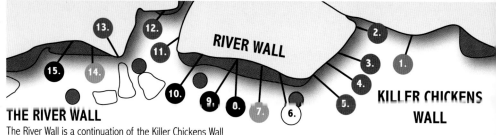

THE RIVER WALL

The River Wall is a continuation of the Killer Chickens Wall and features several challenging routes. This is why you cam to the Promised Land, right?

☐ **6. THE NILE PROJECT (CLOSED)**
Currently a closed project. This route is located 10 feet left of the tree. (Equipped by John Flunker; 6 bolts)

☐ **7. ORANGE (AKA FLOAT TRIP) 5.13A** ★★★
This is the impossible looking line on the wall. Climb through the big crack system up the center of the wall. Shares anchors with **"THE NILE PROJECT."**
(FA John Flunker 2008; 7 bolts)

☐ **8. ZAMBEZI   5.12B** ★★★★
Start 20 feet right of the "MH <3 LH" carved tree on the pod-pocket sharing the start with **"CONGO SPRAY."** At the junction move right. Grab the last good hold out of the short roof and try to catch the sharp, hard-to-see jug as you drive by. This one finishes up on easier terrain.   (FA John Flunker 2007; 6 bolts)

☐ **9. CONGO SPRAY   5.12B** ★★★
Start 20 feet right of the "MH <3 LH" carved tree on the pod-pocket sharing the start with **"ZAMBEZI."** At the junction go left. Climb through hard to see pockets and find the shake at the third bolt. Get ready to hit it hard: superb athletic climbing leads to a "race-the-clock" scenario. Fight to ditch the pump as you make the break for the chains!
(FA Chris Schmick 1998; 6 bolts)

☐ **10. EGYPTIAN CONNIPTION   5.12D** ★★★
Start just left of the "MH <3 LH " tree. This demanding face may not be as steep as the rest, but it takes some serious effort to put this thing down. Climb the left-most line of bolts on the River Wall. (FA John Flunker 2008; 6 bolts)

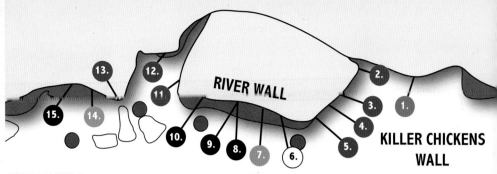

RIVER WALL

KILLER CHICKENS
WALL

TEAM HONDA
The next section of cliff picks up right after the River Wall. **"BETTER LATE THEN NEVER"** 5.11c is on the left side of the River Wall. Be sure to check out the name-sake **"TEAM HONDA"** 5.12A. If 5.12 is you're grade, then step up to the plate on this Jackson Falls classic.

☐ **11. BETTER LATE THAN NEVER** 5.11c
Located on the right side of the alcove is this spectacular and understated line. Commit to a rugged precision move off the ground and keep hustling; this one doesn't let up until the end.
(FA Shawn Watson 1998; 4 bolts)

☐ **12. FASHIONABLY LATE** 5.11A
Located in the alcove uphill from the River Wall, this route begins by laying back on the right-facing flake feature. After clipping the second bolt punch left through incut edges and jugs to reach the anchors. A fantastic hand-over-fist paddle fest!
(FA Shawn Watson 1998, 7 bolts)

☐ **13. CAN'T TAKE THE FUNK** 5.10D
Climb the harder-than-it looks arête to gain the harder-than-it-looks slab, all the while making sure not to blow it at the second or third bolt. It's a lot like a puzzle, but with consequences.
(FA John Flunker 2008; 7 bolts)

☐ **14. PINOCCHIO THEORY** 5.13A
This route tackles the bolt line directly right of **"TEAM HONDA"** and finishes by climbing leftward to join **"TEAM HONDA"** at the 7th bolt.
(FA John Flunker 2008; 8 bolts)

☐ **15 TEAM HONDA** 5.12A
See right.

☐ **15. TEAM HONDA**　　　　**5.12A**

Paddle through sinker holds on the steep face until you reach the break. Recharge here and enjoy even better holds on steeper stone.　(FA Chris Schmick 1998; 7 bolts)

Dan Groves on Team Honda 5.12a. Photo Kevin Sierzega.

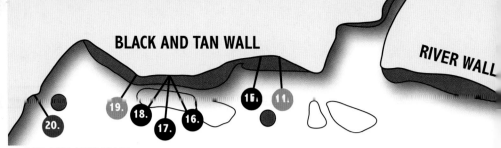

BLACK AND TAN WALL

Routes 16 through 19 are located on the black and tan streaked portion of cliff just left of the Team Honda Wall. These routes do not start from the ground and can be reached by walking along the large, detached platform beneath the wall. It is highly recommended that you stick clip the first bolt before take-off.

☐ **16. POSEUR**   **5.12B** ✭✭✭✭
This is the first route encountered on the large platform beneath the Black and Tan Wall. Clip the first bolt and break right. (FA Shawn Watson 1998; 7 bolts)

☐ **17. HOSER**   **5.12B** ✭✭✭
Clip the first bolt and head left. Power through the middle line on the Black and Tan Wall.
(FA Chris Schmick 1998; 7 bolts)

☐ **18. LAST GASP OF HOPE**   **5.12C** ✭✭✭
See right.

☐ **19. ADIOS AMIGOS**   **5.13B** ✭✭✭
Walk to the far left side of the large platform beneath the Black and Tan Wall until you reach the last line of bolts. Definitely stick-clip the first one; a whip at the start would be treacherous otherwise. Finish on the anchors of **"LAST GASP OF HOPE."** (FA Chris Schmick 1999; 6 bolts)

☐ **20. TRAPLINE**   **5.10B** ✭✭✭
This route starts in front of the tree under the low roof. This long and continuous route features a demanding start. The fight off the ground is well worth it for the technical face climbing above.
(FA Russell Rowlands 1998; 8 bolts)

☐ **18. LAST GASP OF HOPE** 5.12c ★★★
This route follows the left-angling crack. Ride the wave
until it runs out; Finish on the short headwall.
(FA Chris Schmick 1998; 8 bolts)

Jared Smith on Last Gasp of Hope 5.12c. Photo Kevin Sierzega.

MASS PRODUCTION

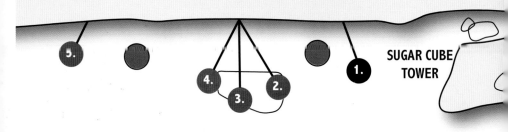

SUGAR CUBE
TOWER

MASS PRODUCTION WALL

☐ **1. ASSEMBLY LINE**   5.12A ⭐⭐
Start just right of the large tree with the big knot. Climb through the right-facing sidepull feature between the 3rd and 4th bolt. (FA Chris Schmick 1999; 6 bolts)

The next three routes share the same start in front of the 5 foot tall talus boulder.

☐ **2. SLAVE LABOR**   5.11B ⭐
Use the shared start and head right to the left-facing flake feature. (FA Russell Rowlands 1998, 6 bolts)

☐ **3. CARPAL TUNNEL**   5.11B ⭐⭐
Use the share start and go straight up through the whitish face. (FA Russell Rowlands 1998; 6 bolts)

☐ **4. WORKSHOP**   5.11C ⭐⭐
Use the shared start and climb left through darker stone. (FA Russell Rowlands 1998; 5 bolts)

☐ **5. BIG CHAW**   5.10B ⭐⭐
Start on the left side of the wall 10 feet left of the S-bend tree. Climb up the orange and gray face through the small roof. (FA Mike Balossi 2002; 4 bolts)

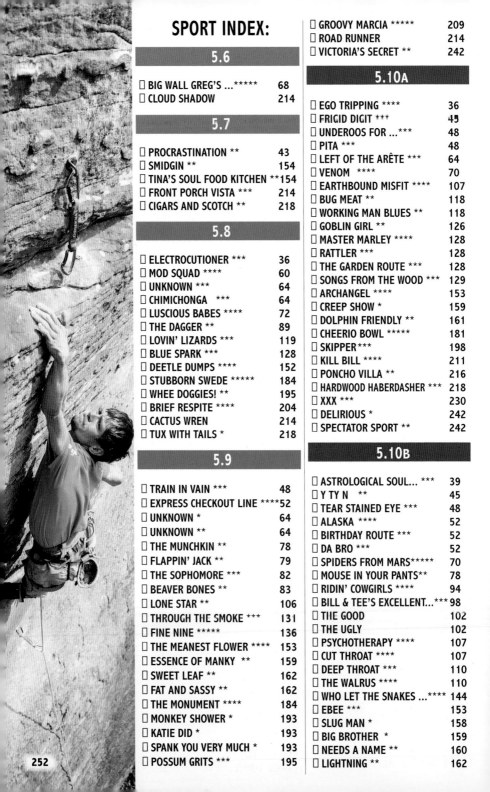

SPORT INDEX:

Photo Jesse Koerner.

GEAR INDEX:

SETTING THE STANDARD™

You know those holds that just feel right? They make sense, they fit the route. Even the tiny crimps are comfortable, the texture always feels perfect, and they are great for training. eGrips start with the best shapers in the game, then use the strongest urethane mix available to pour the holds. Artistry and ergonomics combine for an unmatched experience. eGrips - Setting the Standard.™

Photo Kevin Sierzega.

ALPHABETIC INDEX:

LIST OF NATURAL AREAS:

Atwood Ridge	Ecological area; Research natural area
Ava	Zoological area
Bald Knob	Wilderness area; Geologic area
Barker Bluff	Ecological area; Research natural area
Battery Rock	Heritage resource significant site
Bay Creek	Wilderness area; Candidate wild and scenic river
Bear Creek Relict Site	Botanical area
Bell Smith Springs	Ecological area; National natural landmark
Big Brushy Ridge	Ecological area
Big Creek	Candidate wild and scenic river; Zoological area
Big Grand Pierre Creek	Candidate wild and scenic river
Big Muddy River	Candidate wild and scenic river
Brown's	Zoological area
Bulge Hole	Ecological area
Burden Falls	Wilderness area
Burke Branch	Ecological area; Research natural area
Cane Creek	Botanical area
Caney Branch Barrens	Ecological area
Cave Hill	Ecological area; Research natural area
Chimaphila Site	Botanical area
Clear Creek Swamp	Botanical area
Clear Springs	Geological area; Wilderness area
Copperous Branch	Ecological area
Cretaceous Hills	Ecological area
Crow Knob	Ecological area
Dean Cemetery	Ecological area
Dennison Hollow	Ecological area; Research natural area
Dixon Springs Ag. Center	Intensive research area
Dog Barrens	Ecological area
Double Branch Hole	Ecological area
Dutch Creek Chert Woodland	Ecological area
East Barrens Pine Hills Annex	Ecological area
East Fork Oxalis illinoensis	Botanical area
Fink Sandstone Barrens	Ecological area
Fountain Bluff	Geological area
Garden of the Gods	Wilderness area; Ecological area
Gibbons Creek	Ecological area
Grantsburg Swamp	Ecological area
Greentree Reservoir	Botanical area
Gyp Williams Hollow	Ecological area
Hayes Creek-Fox Den Creek	Ecological area
Hutchins Creek	Candidate wild and scenic river
Hutchison	Zoological area
Illinois Iron Furnace	Heritage resource significant site
Jackson Hole	Ecological area
Jackson Hollow	Ecological area
Kaskaskia Experimental Forest	Intensive research area
Kaskaskia Woods	Ecological area
Keeling Hill North	Ecological area
Keeling Hill South	Ecological area
Kickasola Cemetery	Ecological area
LaRue-Pine Hills/Otter Pond	Ecological area; Research natural area; National natural landmark
Leisure City Barrens	Ecological area
Little Grand Canyon-Horseshoe Bluff	Ecological area; National natural landmark
Lusk Creek	Wilderness area
Lusk Creek	Candidate wild and scenic river; Zoological area
Lusk Creek Canyon	Ecological area; National natural landmark
Lusk Creek North	Ecological area
Martha's Woods	Ecological area
Massac Tower Springs	Ecological area
Millstone Bluff	Ecological area; Heritage resource significant site
Odom Tract	Ecological area
Opossum Trot Trail	Botanical area
Ozark Hill Prairie	Ecological area; Research natural area
Palzo Reclamation Project	Intensive research area
Panther Den	Wilderness area
Panther Hollow	Research natural area; Botanical area
Pleasant Valley Barrens	Ecological area
Poco Cemetery East	Ecological area
Poco Cemetery North	Ecological area
Pounds Hollow	Ecological area
Provo Cemetery	Ecological area
Reddick Hollow	Botanical area
Reid's Chapel	Ecological area
Rich's	Zoological area
Robnett Barrens	Ecological area
Russell Cemetery Barrens	Ecological area
Saline Springs	Heritage resource significant site
Saltpeter Relict	Botanical area
Sand	Ecological area
Schwegman	Ecological area
Silvey Pond	Botanical area
Simpson Township Barrens	Ecological area
Snow Springs	Ecological area
Split Rock Hollow	Ecological area
Stoneface	Ecological area; Research natural area
Sulphur Springs	Botanical area
Teal Pond	Botanical area
Toothless	Zoological area
West Barrens Pine Hollow	Ecological area
Whoopie Cat Mountain	Ecological area; Research natural area
Wolf Creek	Botanical area

Photo Carly Sanders.

ACKNOWLEDGEMENTS AND THANKS

On its surface, this book is a resource for those interested in exploring Southern Illinois climbing. The maps, directions, and descriptions were designed to provide first-time visitors with practical information and suggestions.

It was equally important to create a book for the climbing community that has supported me over the years. I tried, in earnest, to produce something for us to share and look back on together. This book is as much a photo album and collection of short stories as it is a guidebook. For many of us, Jackson Falls has been an important place where our formative years were spent and where many of our strongest relationships were forged.

Climbing added branches to my family tree and I consider myself incredibly fortunate to have such a strong network of friends. Thank you for your help and continued support.

See you out there.

SPECIAL THANKS TO

Sophie Binder	Burke Edwards	John Oungst	Doug Munsch
Patti Zdanowski	Kevin La Forge	David Chancellor	Ian Anderson
Matt Guempel	John Payne	Phillip Carrier	Eric Ulner
Louis Wall	Jessica Joganic	Kevin Sierzega	Paul Hime
John Flunker	Chris & Lauren Loesch	Christopher Andrews	Calvin Hwang
Hannah Ingram	Jeff Frizzell	Jared Smith	Robert Monroe
Carine Doyle	Kevin Todd	Siebert Tregoning	Jacob Teal
Bridget Melloy	Taylor Ashford	Dan Brayack	Kristi Ganz
Aaron Stover	Rob Smith	Ray Ellington	Laura Lecher

YUSUF DANESHYAR

Born and raised in Southern Illinois, Yusuf Daneshyar moved to St. Louis, MO in 2004 to where he was first introduced to climbing. Subsequent years were spent almost exclusively at Jackson Falls- a place that he credits for much, if not all, of his interest in climbing.

Faced with few (read: no) professional opportunities after graduating from the University, Yusuf pursued a career in climbing and traveled extensively throughout North America. His time on the road only validated his opinion that the best sport climbing in the country could be found in a little canyon in Southern Illinois.

More than anything, Yusuf believes that climbing has the ability to open doors for young people,

"Climbing taught me that any goal, personal or professional, is possible. Just like it goes in climbing, sometimes all you need to do is wait for the right conditions, let go of the head games, and most importantly, commit when you find yourself in a position to make that final push for the summit."

AUTHOR
RECOMMENDED ROUTES

Photos Top: Dan Brayack, Right: Aaron Beal.

DAN BRAYACK

Dan Brayack has been climbing for about 18 years and has been a professional climbing photographer for 12 years. Though his scholastic path was bridge engineering, Dan was an editor for his high school yearbook and almost went the Layout and Design path, which has always been one of his passions. He enjoys starting with great images and building a page layout around those images.

Dan has authored the Coopers Rock Bouldering guidebook, and published the Rocktown and Grayson Highlands Bouldering guidebooks (and hopefully if you are reading this - the Jackson Falls Climbing Guidebook.) Dan's primary motivation is to provide for his beautiful little blond dog, Raina who is the love of his life. Dan currently lives in West Virginia near the New River Gorge, his home climbing area... though the Red River Gorge is pretty close!

I would like to thank all of the folks that helped to bring this book together - especially Yusuf who was a pleasure to work with and I think really helped me bring book publishing to the next level. Kevin, thanks so much for everything, it was great talking shop with you with photos and for doing such an excellent job proof reading!

As always my Dad and Grandpa for their support. I swear that I'm not crazy. Bob for always keeping my eyes on the right path (that of the Sith.) My girlfriend (hopefully fiance if she says yes) Lauren, for dealing will obsessive climbing habits. My sponsor - Trango for all the awesome gear and for helping me live my dream of trying to be cool (or at least pretending to be!)

PUBLISHER
RECOMMENDED ROUTES